Glen Jakovich – *Zealous & Bold*

To Richard,
Best Wishes
& Merry Christmas! '2004'

27
WCE.

Printed by Cambridge Media
17 Northwood Street
West Leederville WA 6007 Australia
Tel: (08) 9382 3911   Fax: (08) 9382 3187
Web: www.cambridgemedia.com.au

Text copyright © Gary Stocks 2004

Editorial & Photographic Contributors
Alan East (Editorial & Photographic Consultant)
Ceridwen Clocherty (Editorial & Design Consultant)
Paul Mackey (Design & Layout)
Iain Gillespie (Photographer)
Bill Crabb (Photographer)
Greg Wood (Photographer)
Nadine Wood (Photographer)

National Library of Australia cataloguing data

Stocks, Gary
Glen Jakovich – Zealous & Bold
ISBN 0-9579343-5-1

1.   Sport, Australian Rules Football
2.   Biography
3.   West Australian history

Cover photos
By Ian Gillespie, Courtesy of The West Australian

Contents

Acknowledgements

OVER THE course of my life a number of people have provided me with support, guidance and assistance to get me to where I am today. To Brian Ciccotosto, who encouraged me to fulfil my potential during my junior days at South Coogee and then my journey from colts to senior football for South Fremantle. To Stan Magro, my first senior coach at South Fremantle, who taught me that the most important aspect of football was passion for the jumper, the club and the team. Thanks Stan for all your help at the beginning of my journey. To Peter Sumich and John Worsfold, who also came through South Fremantle and took me under their wing when I joined the West Coast Eagles in 1990. Their influence in shaping my career was and still is paramount. To Trevor Nisbett, whose words of wisdom have helped nurture my career during the good and indifferent times both on and off the field. To Michael Malthouse, who harnessed and developed my footballing talents and continually laid challenges every week for me to aspire to.

To Angie Papodopolous, a terrific manager whose professional acumen and genuine friendship has been greatly appreciated. To Tony Granich, my ex high school teacher whose wisdom, counsel, guidance and friendship continues to this day.

'To my Mum, Allan, Garry, Jodee, Callum and Emilee thank you for all your love and guidance you have provided throughout my life. And to my extended family Tony, Stefica and Anthony Petkovich and Tania and Tony Marraffa thanks for your support and direction over the years. And to the 'crew' and all my close friends thanks for your encouragement and friendship.'

To Emely, my wife, my love, my confidante, my soulmate, my strength who has been with me through the highs and lows of my football career but has given me the greatest gift – my two daughters Anique and Jayda.

Glen Jakovich

Author's Acknowledgements

I would like to acknowledge and thank the many people who have assisted with the compilation of this book. First and foremost I appreciate the opportunity that Glen Jakovich gave me to be involved when he wandered into my office one day towards the end of the 2003 season and asked if I could help write this account of his life and his career. He has been a wonderful player, as evidenced by the glowing list of achievements, and it has been a pleasure to watch him play the game, initially as a journalist and more recently in my role as communications manager with the West Coast Eagles Football Club.

To the many people who also gave of their time to share their experiences, both on and off the field, I thank them for making themselves available and for providing a variety of perspectives on the man himself. To Mary, Allan and Emely Jakovich as well as Tony Granich thank you for that insight. To former teammate and current coach John Worsfold, respected opponents Wayne Carey and Stephen Kernahan as well as long-time South Fremantle administrator Brian Ciccotosto it was a pleasure to discuss your personal experiences with Glen.

In his life it is doubtful whether any man did more to shape both the player and the individual than former coach Mick Malthouse. I would like to thank and acknowledge Mick for his time and effort. Another person who has played a significant role in moulding Glen has been Trevor Nisbett, both as football manager and now as chief executive of the West Coast Eagles. His support for this project and his guidance was greatly appreciated.

I would also like to thank Ray Wilson, sports editor, Paula Rogers and Iain Gillespie, all from The West Australian, for their valuable assistance. Ray has and will give the book great editorial support, Paula has been a wonderful ally in providing the distribution mechanism for getting the book into the market place and Iain's work is there for us all to see in the cover and back page photographs. Other important photographic support came through Greg and Nadine Wood and Bill Crabb, the official West Coast Eagles photographer.

Finally I would like to acknowledge the contribution of two people for making this book what it is, a publication I modestly suggest will be judged as being both an entertaining and interesting read. Alan East, a long time mentor and respected colleague, provided valuable direction and editing of the book while the efforts of Ceri Clocherty and the team at Cambridge Media were, as always, of the highest order.

It was a pleasure to be involved in writing Jako: Zealous and Bold and I anticipate that all of those people who have played their part in its compilation will share my pride in the finished product.

Gary Stocks

About the author

GARY STOCKS is an award-winning journalist who spent 25 years working in newspapers before joining the West Coast Eagles as Communications Manager in 2000.

The last 18 years of his journalistic career were spent as a football writer with *The West Australian* where he was regularly honoured at the annual Football Media Guild Awards. In 1998 he won the Gilmour Prize for the best piece of sports reporting in WA through the Australian Journalists' Association and his most cherished achievement was in 2000 when he won the Football Media Guild's annual presentation, the Geoff Christian Award for football writing excellence.

Stocks had the privilege of working for a number of years with Mr Christian, the doyen of football journalists and an inaugural inductee into the WA Football Hall of Fame and a member of the AFL Hall of Fame. Stocks' last assignment with *The West Australian* was to cover the Sydney Olympic Games in 2000.

Zealous and bold

THE MOTTO on our family crest states in Latin *Sedulus et Audax*. Translated it means *zealous and bold*.

I believe that this motto encapsulates my family's values and view on life and none more so than that of my late Father Darko. He left the island of Solta in Yugoslavia now Croatia with nothing more than a suitcase to come to Australia to earn a better lifestyle and to offer better opportunities for his family. The hardships that he endured and the risks that he took, like so many other migrants of his day, are at times difficult to comprehend for children of migrant parents.

His daring to leave Croatia and all that he knew and his boldness to lay his roots in what was then rural Wattleup and start a market garden business, to my mind, is an incredible feat. In many ways, he was a zealot whose sole aim was to better the lives of himself and his future family. Through sweat, blood and tears, he and Mum raised three boys, ran a successful market garden business and provided me with the values and ethics that I hold dear to this day.

Thus, this book is dedicated to my late Father Darko, the boldest and most zealous man I have ever known.

Glen Jakovich

Foreword

Single-minded determination

IN MY TIME in AFL football I have seen many players driven by an intense desire to succeed. However, I doubt if I have seen anyone more determined than Glen Jakovich.

Like everyone who reaches the pinnacle of their sport, Glen had to overcome a few setbacks along the way. Initially, there was some uncertainty as to whether the West Coast Eagles would draft him and then he had to bide his time for his chance at senior football. For most of us, 10 weeks of playing WAFL football while waiting for an opportunity at the higher level would not be too excruciating, but for Glen that was extremely difficult. He was dominating the local competition, but couldn't get his chance at the higher level.

While Glen and I were both from South Fremantle, I didn't know him when I was playing with the Bulldogs. I knew his brother Allan pretty well, because I played club football and Teal Cup with him, but Glen was a couple of years younger. However, when he first arrived at the West Coast Eagles, there was that link between Glen, Peter Sumich and myself because we all came from South. When Glen joined the club, he looked up to us because he'd seen us come through and watched us playing as kids as well. We used to call him 'the young bloke' and, because he was the apprentice, so to speak, he was our designated driver. He was coming from further south, so he picked us up on the way through for training or the airport; things like that.

He had to earn his stripes in where he sat, not just in the footy club, but with Suma and myself. He'd pick the car up, park the car, carry the bags – we just found him as a kid who just wanted to succeed. He was hungry and prepared to do absolutely everything to get the best out of himself to succeed. Part of that for him was to learn from senior players or players already playing AFL football to see what we knew and what it took to play at the level.

In 1991 his form at South Fremantle was exceptional, but he had to wait about 10 weeks before getting his chance. While he never questioned authority over his non-selection, I know that within himself he would have been more determined by the week to make it harder and harder for the selectors to leave him out. Knowing Glen, I'm sure he would have just been saying to himself "I will just keep working hard, keep my head down and work hard." As much as he might have been desperate for an opportunity, it wouldn't have changed his focus on what he was doing.

In playing with Glen and the other blokes in the West Coast Eagles defence, there was a strong bond between us all. With Glen, Guy McKenna, Michael Brennan, David Hart, Dwayne Lamb and Ashley McIntosh, there was an extremely strong bond. At times, Mitchell White and Chris Waterman were part of that as well.

Throughout his career, Glen set himself apart from other centre half-backs through his ability to dominate his position and dominate his opponent, not just defend his opponent – and to really attack as well. For a centre half-back to win the number of possessions that he's won over his whole career is very, very good. He has that outstanding ability to read the game, to back himself. It got to be tough for sides because some tried to take Bluey McKenna out of the game and others tried to take Jako out of the game. That really affected the way rivals wanted to play. If they had a good centre half-forward and didn't want to play him there, that eliminated one of their strengths as well.

We had a pretty good mix in defence because we just knew how to cover for each other. Nine out of 10 marking contests I was in, I would spoil, whereas Bluey might spoil six out of 10 and go for four marks. We knew how to read each other with that. When I was in a contest, Bluey or the other guys would know to run and crumb the spoil, whereas, if Bluey were involved, we might run down the ground earlier and get in position to receive the ball from him because we had faith that if he decided to mark it, he would mark it. With Glen, we also knew how he would operate. He would spoil if he had to, mark it if he could but, more often than not, he'd try to anticipate what was unfolding further up the ground and intercept the ball before it got to his opponent.

He's had a wonderful career and when he retires he will retire as the games record holder at our club. Clearly he is one of the truly great players to represent the West Coast Eagles and was pivotal in the club's greatest triumphs.

John Worsfold

The early days

Convincing Darko

GLEN JAKOVICH was just six years old, but he knew what he wanted. However, every time he sought permission from his father to play Australian Football, the request was rejected. Typically that rejection was greeted by tears; Glen responded the way any kid would do when told he wouldn't get his own way.

As the football world has come to know, Jakovich is nothing if not determined and he continued to ask the question before eventually receiving the answer he sought. He wanted to follow elder brothers Gary and Allan into the Australian game, while his father Darko had a more genteel sport in mind. Yet, perhaps sensing that he was fighting a losing cause, Jakovich senior relented – and for that the football world should be eternally grateful.

"I was getting to the age where I wanted to play junior football," Jakovich recounted. "My first hurdle was my father because he didn't want us playing football, he preferred soccer or a non-contact sport, but Mum tried to soften him up. Gary and Allan were older and already playing. There are five years between Gary and Allan and another five years between Allan and I, so I enjoyed watching them play on a Sunday and that's where I got the passion to play footy.

"Growing up in the district that we did, football was the only game. We loved to watch the ABC show *The Winners* and, admiring my brothers as I did, saw me gravitate towards football. My brothers were playing at the South Coogee Junior Football Club and I was only six at the time. Back then, the South Coogee jumper was the St Kilda strip. Dad could see how badly I wanted to play because each time I asked and he said 'no' I cried. Mind you, I was only grade one, but finally he let me play when I was seven.

"I went to South Coogee Primary School and the South Coogee Football Club oval was close by, so I would go to training straight after school and wait for Mum and Dad to pick me up, or I would get a lift with the parents of one of the kids in my class.

"I played soccer at school, but not a lot. No-one played soccer, everyone played footy, but because there were a lot of ethnics in our school, every now and again we played soccer. But football was dominant because we all went to watch South Fremantle play."

That link to community football has long been the core of the great Australian game; it's the very reason why it has been dubbed the people's game. Part of the tradition at WAFL level has been the assembly of kids behind the goals, waiting for a ball to sail over the fence so they could contest the ball on the bank. Of course, there was also an underlying motivation of perhaps grabbing a 'souvenir' from a game. It was on those banks at Fremantle Oval that the Jakovich boys honed their skills and developed their passion for the game. South Fremantle might have lost a couple of footballs along the way, but it proved a wonderful investment, both for their club and the game generally.

"Dad and his group of friends he migrated with loved South Fremantle and would go down and watch the games," Jakovich recounted. "We would sit behind the goals waiting for the ball to be kicked through. Then we'd fight for the footy on the bank, try to grab it and race home with it or kick it back through the goals. If it went too far over the bank, the footy rarely came back. One of the kids would take off with it and have a brand new Burley to kick around.

"If you wanted to play footy you had to knock off a ball and we knocked off a few footies along the way. To buy a new footy was 30 or 40 bucks and we couldn't afford that... I remember Allan getting one from South Fremantle that was kicked into the crowd. He marked it and jumped the fence to Fremantle Hospital and bolted. I knew he was going to do that because we'd often talked about it. I met him down at the bus stop, but the old

With Darko Jakovich being of Croatian extraction, soccer was his game of choice and that was the code he wanted his sons to play. But, one by one, they took to the Australian game. Gary had already converted to Aussie Rules when his parents and three-year-old brother, Glen, went to Croatia on holiday. The two eldest boys were left behind and, at that stage, Allan was playing soccer.

"We were only in Croatia for about three weeks and we were sent a cutting out of the local paper – Allan was listed as the best player in a football game," Mary said. "That was the start of Allan's football career and, a few years later, Glen convinced his Dad to allow him to play. Glen achieved success pretty early, but I was never concerned that he might be thrown in at the deep end. I left that to the coaches, I thought they wouldn't do the wrong thing by him so I left it to them. All of the boys were good players, but also very different people. Allan is a good kid, people get the wrong impression of him sometimes. Allan did like going out, while Glen was very dedicated to his football and he wouldn't come home late at night, he wouldn't go out if he was playing the next day, he wouldn't eat the wrong food."

Mary Jakovich

man wanted to stay and watch the rest of the game. Allan couldn't hide it anywhere, so he just hung on to it. We didn't care about the result, we just couldn't wait to get home to kick the league footy around. That was one of our great memories, coming home and playing under lights in the backyard with an official Burley football. We got a few of them over the years but, after the club had lost a few too many, they put a security guard near the Mr Whippy van, which was right next to the bar. Any kid trying to jump the fence with a footy was nabbed.

"I guess when people ask me when did I make up my mind to play league footy, it was those times going to Fremantle Oval, watching South play, watching the great Aboriginal contingent play – Stephen Michael, Maurice Rioli, Benny Vigona, Michael Cockie, Willie Roe and then Noel Carter, Paul Vasoli, Wayne Delmenico, Ray Bauskis, Joe McKay and Jamie Lockyer. Lockyer was the Warwick Capper back then. Kevin Cornell, Paul Mountain, I knew them all, had all their autographs.

"After the game you would try and sneak into the change rooms. I remember Hank Gloede, who was the propertyman, was always kicking me in the butt. Players used chewies before a game in those days and he nabbed me one day when I tried to pinch some. He still remembers that. It was funny because he's the propertyman at the West Coast Eagles. That was when I decided I wanted to wear one of those red and white jumpers.

"I had a great connection with the game from a young age, through my school, the South Coogee Junior Football Club and South Fremantle, going every week to watch the home games or catching a bus or train, or both, to Bassendean or Subiaco, wherever South were playing. Bassendean was a long trip, even Subiaco was a long way. But we were proud and passionate South Fremantle supporters and wanted to be at their games. They were my early memories and from there I just had a real passion to play and I just loved playing."

Schoolyard outcasts

MANY THINGS have changed in the Australian mindset over the last couple of decades – one of them has been the evolution of our nation as multi-cultural. Generally there is now a greater acceptance of people, ideas and beliefs from other cultures. When the Jakovich family was running a market garden to sustain itself 25 years ago, things were different. Before the boys headed off to school they had already done a couple of hours' work, cultivating the vegetables, and they were often targeted because of that.

"We would be working in the market garden, always bare foot and we worked pretty hard," Jakovich recalled. "My father was pretty sick and, with a family to support and feed and no trade or qualifications, we ran a market garden.

"He had a chronic back problem which required two major operations, one in the mid '70s and one later on, so the strain of lifting boxes and potato sacks and driving tractors took [its] toll. It was hard work on the old man just to live and support his kids.

"I was working in the market garden from seven years of age, doing whatever I could. Whether that was picking crops or harvesting onions or carrots, picking tomatoes... obviously I didn't do any of the heavy stuff because Dad didn't want me to injure my back like he had. Dad had us up at the crack of dawn from an early age and we put in a couple of hours before school. At that stage we used to get teased a bit because we weren't like the normal Australian family. I used to go to school and my hands would stink of onions or garlic cloves and we used to cop a bit. We were looked upon as outcasts and the other kids thought our father was a real hard bastard. He was, but he was also a great family man.

"We used to work in the garden on the weekends when other kids would ride to the beach or go down the park and have a kick. But, in our lunch breaks, or when the old man went

In later years, when the brothers were playing elite footy, there was no handicap system in place to equalise the contest and nor should there have been. But growing up, with a five year spread between each of the Jakovich clan, there needed to be ways to balance the games.

"I had to bat left-handed," Allan said. "I taught myself to bat left-handed, played a couple of games like that and batted myself into being a left-hander. I reckon he ruined a good cricket career, as I still rate myself as one of the all-time great backyard cricketers! While I bat left-handed, I play right-handed at golf."

Allan Jakovich

While Glen Jakovich's on-field achievements have been well documented, his private life has mirrored his football accomplishments. He did things on a football field well ahead of his time – that was also his life away from the public glare.

When most kids in their mid-teens were riding bikes to the beach, he was doing his bit in the family market garden. When young men of his vintage were enjoying life's social aspects, Jakovich remained at home, giving himself his best chance of success in the game. Committed to his family and to his own goals, his biggest fan, both as a player and a person is his mother, Mary.

"He's been a great son," she said, that sense of pride obvious as a smile swept across her face. "He was doing more than his share from a young age. On weekends, his mates used to ride through on their bikes on their way to the beach and he would be picking tomatoes.

"He was very close to his Dad and they would often go fishing and then cook the fish together; he always watched his Dad, who taught him everything.

"I was born here, but my husband was born in Croatia and I wanted the boys to speak Croatian, so Gary, my eldest, couldn't speak English when he first went to school; not one word, but within a couple of weeks he was.

"The children were five years apart, so Glen and Allan were taught by Gary how to speak English and were able to do that when they went to school. I thought that when they were playing outside they could speak English, but at home they learnt Croatian and they appreciate that now. Glen loves it over there.

"The three of them were sports champions of their year and now my grand children are doing it. Gary had problems with both knees. South Fremantle begged him to have the problem operated on and said they would get him the best surgeons, but Gary was frightened.

"Knee surgery back then wasn't what it is like today. It broke his heart, but then he went into diving."

Mary Jakovich

down to the markets, we would grab a footy and have a kick in the paddock. If it was summer time we pulled out the cricket bat. Once Dad returned, we went back to work. He didn't mind, I think he admired our passion because all three of us were very, very competitive.

"We used to make our own cricket bats, saw them down to size and we went through a few by breaking them or throwing them. We used garden gloves for wicket-keeping and batting. We drew a crease with chalk, devised our own runs system and, like most other backyard games, we'd have our own Test match. Allan and I used to play one out, two out; I'd have to get him out once, but he'd have to get me out twice just because of the age difference.

"It was three out, five out or five out, 10 out if it was a really big match. There was always the odd blue, because that was our competitive nature. And I guess the older brothers are always trying to pull the wool over your eyes and I could see through that. I would try and stand up for myself, but lost about 95 percent of the time just because of the age gap. It was healthy rivalry and, as I look back, they were the best days of my life. It was a strict up bringing but, while Dad was very hard, he was fair. At the time we felt disadvantaged because the other kids had beaut new things, new push bikes and all the latest gear. But if we didn't make it ourselves, we'd get hold of most things somehow.

The football dream

ALL West Coast Eagles fans have seen it – that pure joy Glen Jakovich displays after kicking a goal. It's the raw passion and excitement that goes with success; the same passion that surfaced after Australia beat Ireland at Subiaco Oval in a hybrid rules match at the end of the 2003 season. The crowds were minuscule by comparison and so was the young man, but the genesis for those displays of unbridled enthusiasm emanated from the South Coogee Football Club. Jakovich has always loved playing the game and enjoyed showing it.

"When I was young I was taller than most of the other kids," he said. "But my enthusiasm was always my greatest asset, right from day one. Where other kids might be a bit reserved and sit back and wait, I'd get the footy; chase it down myself.

"At the time, St Kilda were a lowly side, usually sitting near the bottom of the ladder and South Coogee wore the same colours. We couldn't compete with Cockburn and Hilton Park, where players like Brad Hardie, Peter Sumich and John Worsfold were from. They would kick 34.20 to our 1.4 or something like that. But that was our district, a good little community. My brothers obviously played there as well, so did Warren Mosconi, who played a lot with South Fremantle and for WA and his brother Danny. After me there was Travis Gaspar, but by then the club had re-located to Sandridge Park where the boom housing development took off. South Coogee is now a power club and Cockburn and Hilton Park are struggling.

You often hear of junior coaches warning of the dangers of over-exposing young players to their chosen sport. They preach the ill-effects of burn-out; how playing too much and being solely focused on their sport can be their undoing... by their late teens, many outstanding young sports stars are lost to their field. Glen Jakovich was an exception; he had an insatiable appetite for the game and would play at any opportunity.

"We worked out one year that he played 64 games of football," says South Fremantle's general manager Brian Ciccotosto. "With his school commitments, State trial games for the Teal Cup and playing State schoolboys, he had about three games a week. He went to Canberra with the Teal Cup and then played State schoolboys. Greg Brehaut coached the Teal Cup team and they didn't play Jako first up. I said to them 'the boy can play, don't bring him all the way over without playing him.' They did play him after that and he had a pretty good carnival.

"When I sat down with Jako at the end of that season he knew every game he had played. He could tell you who it was against and how he had played, but I said to him there is this thing called a burn-out factor! I said it mightn't affect you now, but it could later on. Well, he has played 270 games of AFL footy and another 60-odd for us, so it doesn't look as thought it has had much effect on him!"

Brian Ciccotosto

"I see a few kids I used to play with every now and again when I go to Fremantle. If I go into the Newport Hotel in the off-season for a quiet beer and a game of pool, I'll run into them and have a bit of a chat. It's 23 years on, but good to catch up with them."

After his initial introduction with South Coogee, Jakovich soon found himself vying for selection in representative teams.

"I started playing combined under-12s and I was picked in the combined 14s and 16s teams, from where they picked the State schoolboys side. We had a district carnival to help pick the Schoolboys side and my first two games weren't crash hot. But, in my last game, I went to the backline and played really well before they picked a squad of 42 for the schoolboys side. I didn't expect to make it because I didn't have a flash carnival, but I was home on the tractor when I got a phone call from one of the ladies at South Coogee telling me I'd been selected in the State squad.

"I nearly dropped, I couldn't believe it. Mine was the last name read out from a list of 42. Rick Evans was the coach and he put me in the 42, but they had to trim it back to 25 and

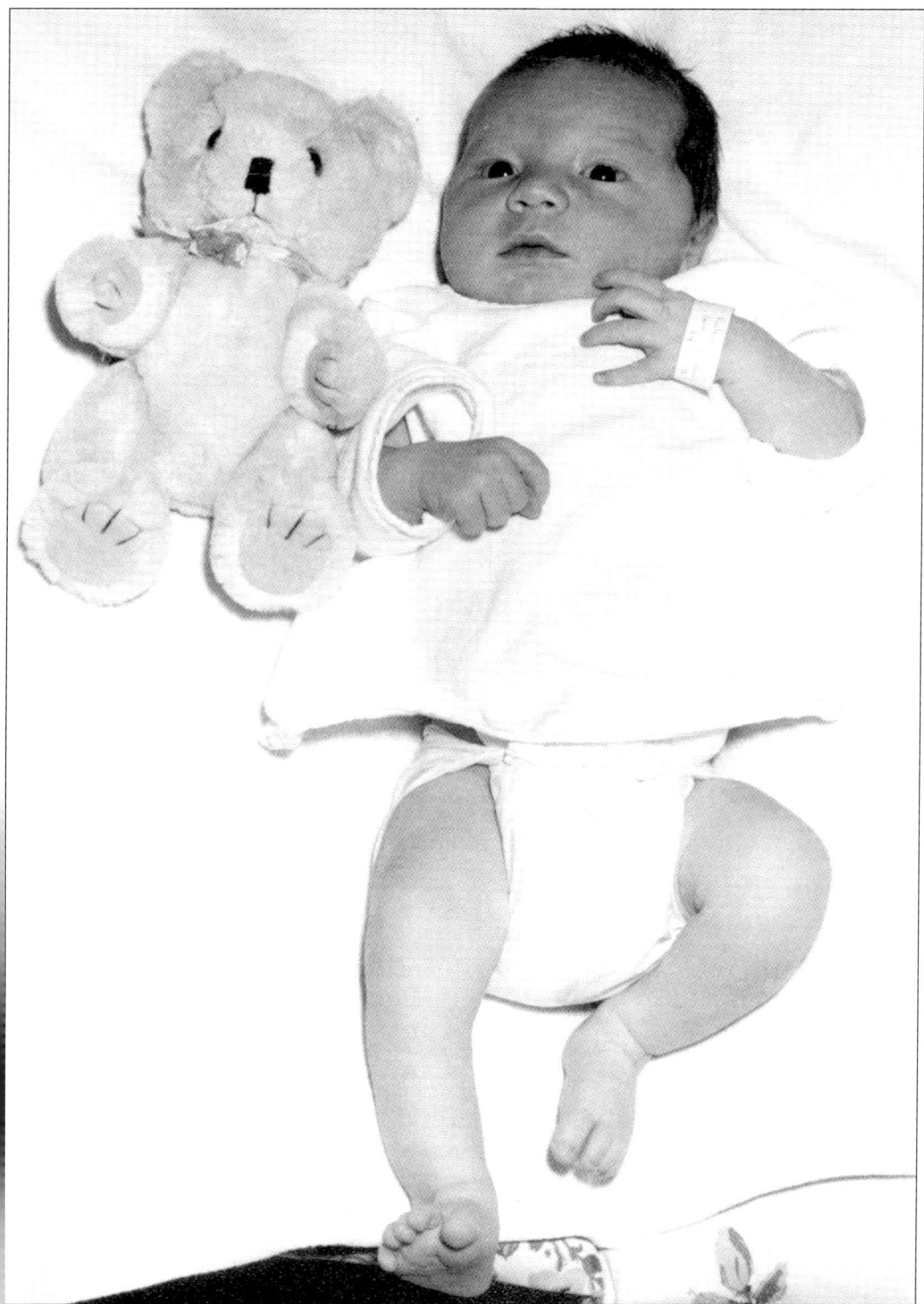

Baby Glen.

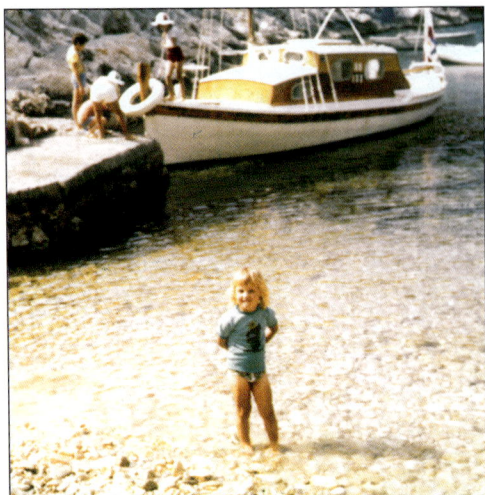
On the pebbled beach in Solta, Croatia.

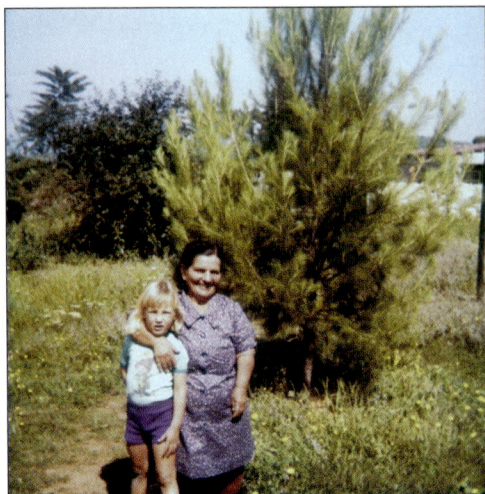
His first visit back to Croatia as a three-year-old.

Allan, Glen and Gary in their youth.

Cute as a button…Glen the toddler takes time out on the lounge room floor.

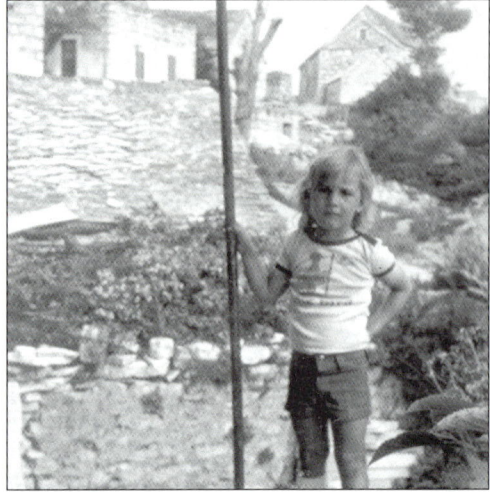

Another happy snap from the visit to Croatia.

God parents Frank Elezovich and Linda Bond
with Glen at his christening.

An early memory of his school days.

A magnificent skippy on show after an early
fishing expedition.

Rare feat... Mary is flanked by Allan (South Australia) and Glen (Western Australia) before they clashed in a 1990 State game.

The Jakovich boys, Allan (left), Glen and Gary bid farewell to their father.

Young gun…Glen accepts his tracksuit as part of the presentation ceremony for his Teal Cup selection.

Glen shares a wonderful moment in his career with his mother Mary after the 1992 grand final.

Family pride... Glen with proud parents after he had earned Teal Cup selection.

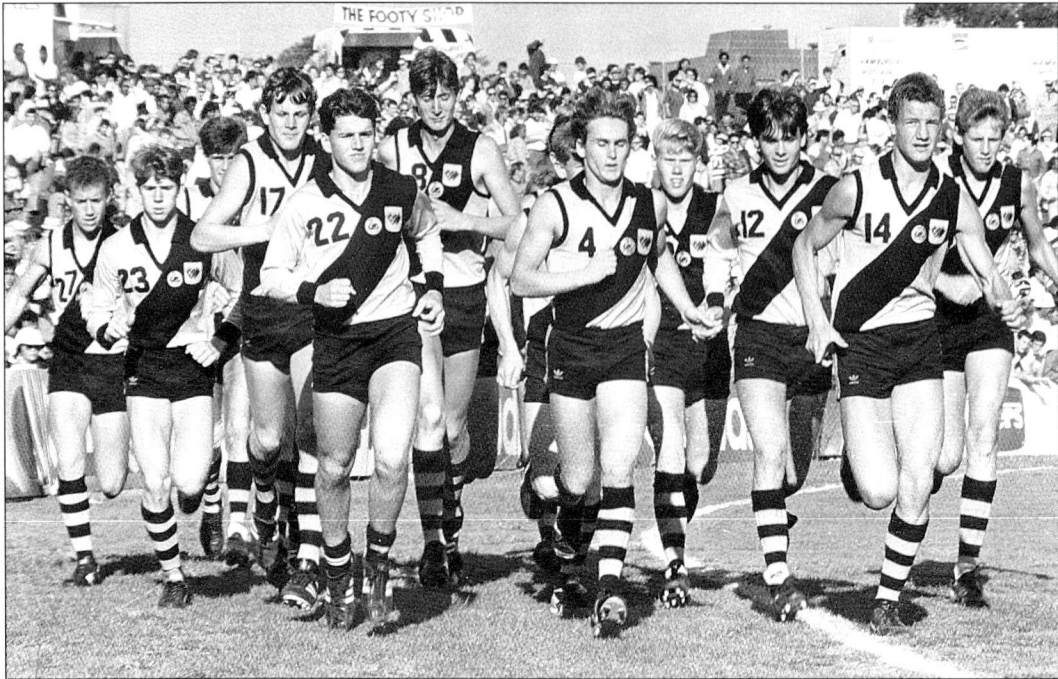

The 1987 State Schoolboys team embarks on a lap of honour of Subiaco Oval.

No quitters... Hamilton Senior High School won the Quit Cup from 1987 - 1989 and this is the last of those victorious teams.

Stars in waiting... Jakovich takes off his boots while Stevan Jackson and Peter Matera have a cooling ale.

Jakovich marks in front of Swan Districts' Kim Hetherington.

Jakovich and Willie Rioli who later played for Hawthon lead a triumphant South team off the ground.

State of Origin selection in 1996.

Getting ready to leave Perth to represent his State in the schoolboys competition in 1988.

With Mick Malthouse in 1991 when WA won the national championship.

Getting ready to fire out a handpass.

Ready to fly as an Eagle.

An early battle with Carlton champion Stephen Kernahan.

Glory bound... Jakovich makes his way onto the MCG for the 1992 grand final.

Earning attention...Jakovich chats with Caroline Wilson, a reporter with The Age newspaper in Melbourne.

Jakovich in the media spotlight as he leaves Subiaco Oval after a battle with Footscray. Daniel Southern, the anti-hero of the clash in 1994, is obviously amused.

Sizing up his options...Jakovich looks downfield during a game against Hawthorn.

that's when I realised I was reasonably good at the game, getting some recognition by making the State squad. I was still eligible for another year, but I made the 25 after a series of practice matches at Perth Oval. From the 42 they picked two teams and put them up against each other. In my first game I played in the forward line and just ran all over the ground and kicked five goals. I was determined to show them I could play.

"I went well in the scratch matches and they picked 30 players to go to a training camp at Penrhos College, which was a five-day live-in camp; at the end of it they had to trim another five. I survived the cut, the championships were held here and I was pick No.14. It was quite

The five-year difference in age between the brothers meant that the senior brother saw precious little of his kid brother's formative years. When Glen was playing junior footy, Allan was occupied with his own career which was starting to blossom at South Fremantle and included a place in the first WA Teal Cup team to win the national championship in 1985. He played alongside that 'Magnificent Seven' of West Coast players-to-be, Worsfold, McKenna, Peter Sumich, Chris Lewis, Scott Watters, Chris Waterman and Paul Peos, in probably the most talented youth team ever to represent the State.

"My first recollection of Glen playing football was when he came down for a junior carnival at Fremantle," Allan reflected. "He was playing centre half-back and was a head taller than most other kids. He was probably 12 or 13 at the time and one thing that has always stuck in my mind was that I just couldn't believe the way he went about his football; his second and third efforts. I didn't learn about those things until well into my senior career but, even at that age, Glen was a player who just kept competing for the ball, doing everything he could to win possession. He was just so determined.

"I am not a believer in natural ability. You only get to be good at something through hours and hours of practice. Sure, you have some God-given talent, but then you have to hone those skills through practice. I was astounded at the second and third efforts of Glen, the smothering, the work ethic and the discipline. I was pre-occupied with kicking goals and used to practise that all the time, but Glen concentrated on other things.

"Glen was obviously the youngest and he had an understanding at a very young age of what he needed to do to be successful. He was driven by a desire to succeed. It wasn't until he was playing Teal Cup that I really saw how much ability he had and he carried a sense of desperation with him, a determination to succeed.

Allan Jakovich

nerve-wracking because five guys had to miss out. Jason Norrish played, Lee Walker was in that team as well and he was an All-Australian."

Jakovich has an amazing ability to recall events with great accuracy and that initial State schoolboys carnival is clearly something he cherishes.

"I had a pretty good carnival. I kicked 27.25, so I had 52 shots at goal in seven games because we played all the other States and Territories. We came equal first and beat Victoria on the opening day – I kicked 4.6 in that game."

After playing so well in that carnival, Jakovich was almost guaranteed a place the following year when he was vice-captain to Walker – a brilliant young athlete whose career was tragically cut short by a series of knee injuries. Walker later joined Jakovich at the West Coast Eagles, but didn't play a game before moving to Collingwood, where he notched a handful of matches before again being cut down by injury. Both Walker and Jakovich were also selected in the WA Teal Cup team that same year.

"I was vice-captain in the second season, but Lee Walker broke his arm in the second game," Jakovich said. "The schoolboys championships were played in Tasmania and we were billeted out and I was lucky to get the general manager of CUB, who is a Geelong board member and I still stay in touch with him.

It was supposed to be a day off; a break from the interstate rivalry at the State schoolboys championships in Hobart in 1988. As it transpired, it simply became a battle of a different kind and the venue, rather than being one of Hobart's picturesque football grounds, was a snow covered Mt Wellington.

"We had a day off and all the teams went to Mt Wellington," Jakovich recalled. "It wasn't organised as a group trip but, as it turned out, each State made the excursion independently and we all ended up there together. It was minus three degrees and snowing and this almighty snowball fight broke out among the States. We were in bunkers, behind monuments and walls, throwing snow at each other. It was great fun, we were all in our teams and it just took one bloke to throw a bit of snow and it was on – State against State. There was great passion and humour.

"When we were up there we could see the whole of Hobart spread out below and it was a lovely tourist attraction. Only a few boys from the Northern Territory, West Australia and South Australia had seen snow before, so it was a bit of a novelty for all of us."

Glen Jakovich

"Ralph Shanahan and his wife Loretta lived in Blackman's Bay, which is like Cottesloe, and they looked after me like you wouldn't believe. Later, when the West Coast Eagles beat Geelong in those grand finals, he would always ring me. As it turned out, I won best and fairest for WA and was runner-up in the national medal on the way to winning All-Australian selection, which was a big thrill.

"We had played in the Teal Cup in Canberra before the State schoolboys and I was determined to do well because the Teal Cup was disappointing. I suppose I was lucky; there were two 15-year-olds doing really well and I was also playing colts footy for South at the time. I played only two of the four matches in Canberra and that's why I wanted to go to Hobart and do well. Lee was an All-Australian Teal Cup player as a 15-year-old... in that carnival Wayne Carey, Robert Harvey, Jose Romero and Corey Young all played."

Perhaps that was the start of the Carey-Jakovich rivalry, while Young famously played just the one game for West Coast after questioning coach Mick Malthouse at one of the breaks.

The first steps to success

Strange as it may seem, even an exceptional young player like Glen Jakovich was initially unsure whether he had the makings of a successful football career until he started to succeed in under-age State teams. After being the last player selected in a 42-strong State schoolboys squad as a 15-year-old, to playing Teal Cup and schoolboys in the same season a year later, Jakovich began to dream about the possibilities ahead. He started to think about playing league football for South Fremantle and perhaps moving into the VFL. He didn't realise, however, how quickly his dream would materialise.

"After going into the Schoolboys squad as the 42nd player and then, a year later, playing Teal Cup, that was when I earmarked a career for myself in football," Jakovich said. "We went to Canberra for the 1989 Teal Cup carnival and played in muddy conditions, the only green bit being the fringe of grass around the goal posts.

"A few good players were involved in that carnival, including one of the brilliant Krakouer boys, who was an All-Australian. I only played two of the four games while, in contrast, Lee Walker excelled and was our No.1 ruckman after another big man was injured. Despite the rather disappointing carnival, I was an automatic selection for the State schoolboys championships. Lee was also an automatic selection. I was determined to have a good carnival and I think we finished third. I was runner-up for the competition's best-player medal and was WA's fairest and best. Jason McCartney played in that carnival and was an All-Australian after being a dominant player for Victoria. He and I became good friends as our careers followed similar paths. He was a year younger than me, but we played Teal Cup and then corresponding carnivals after that."

While committed to his State, Jakovich also remained loyal to his school's cause and Hamilton Hill Senior High School was enjoying a strong run of success. It seemed Jakovich simply could not get enough football.

"Brian Gray coached four premierships in five years at Hammy Hill, the CIG Shield and Quit Cup," Jakovich spruiked. "We had a dominant school, I played 72 games of football in one year and, the year before, when I was 14, I played 68 games. That was State schoolboys, the Teal Cup, all the trial games and curtain-raisers before the Eagles matches, which were a great highlight of mine.

"Some people were worried about my workload, but they weren't going to stop me. My school needed me and why wouldn't you want to play for your school? We were playing a curtain-raiser to an Eagles game and that was a great opportunity to play in front of 30,000 people.

"We beat Mazenod College at Subiaco Oval and beat Warwick in the Barry Cable Division final. Michael Dunstan played, as did Preston Holland, Nicky Bolton, Danny D'Angelo and Tommy Bottrell, who also played at South Fremantle. Paul Symmons, later to be an Eagles teammate, played for Warwick, while Bruce McKnight played for Mazenod and went on to play for East Perth and South. I played Teal Cup with Bruce, so there were some pretty good players coming through at the time."

Along life's journey, we all meet people who influence our lives enormously; people who provide direction and counsel when it is most needed; people who become life-long friends. Glen Jakovich had no idea at the time but, when he began Year 8 at Hamilton Hill Senior High School in 1986, his life path crossed and then connected with a young man who had just graduated from university. Tony Granich and Jakovich gelled immediately, a bond that was forged by a love of football and a similar family background. They remain close friends today. Here is an account of their relationship by Tony Granich.

"My first recollection of Glen was at a Delta sub-school meeting in December 1985. The agenda item was the incoming Year 8s and, in particular, Glen Jakovich and Paul Cassetai. To a young first-year-out teacher, these two boys were demonised as Perth's equivalent to the Kray brothers. Discussion focussed on how to behaviourally manage these boys and not allow Glen to get away with what Allan did. To me, it appeared that a few old scores were to be settled at Glen's expense. This would not be the first time Glen would take the brunt for Allan and stand up for the family name. Anyway, Glen was placed in my social studies class and I looked forward to seeing him next year. Maybe it was idealism and my belief that he couldn't be that bad.

"The first time I met Glen was in February 1986; he stood out because he was the biggest kid in the class. To my surprise, he sat up the front and didn't say a word. When I called the roll, he responded politely, but what I read in his posture and body language was a kid who was quite scared, even unsure of himself. I looked him in the eye and he seemed to recoil a bit. It gave the impression of a kid asking 'what have I done?' I looked down at his desk and on his file he had a picture of a Carlton footballer. I was and still am a fanatical Carlton supporter. I said to Glen 'So you barrack for the Blues'. He said 'yeah'. I replied 'We will get on famously'. Glen smiled and I just moved on reading the roll.

"To me, Glen felt like he had an ally; someone in authority who would actually give him a chance. His other teachers apparently harked on about how bad Allan was and that Glen would be paying the price for his brother's sins. So it was with relief that Glen came to my classes. We developed a relationship based on football. I had played football for Subiaco and could relate to his dreams of being a footballer. We would discuss training schedules that I endured, styles of players, best players, a whole range of topics based around experiences and perceptions. This helped his school work because he was enthusiastic to do well in my class. We also had the same cultural background which bonded us. In the '80s you still felt like a 'wog'. We had a connection, like a sixth sense about certain situations that arose at school. I went an extra yard for all students, but in particular for kids like Jako.

"Because of our relationship, Glen and I would talk about lots of issues that affected him. The politics of Yugoslavia, family, values, friendships, school life and, of course, football were always subjects at the forefront of our discussions.

"To dispel a myth, Glen was not as bad academically as some make out. He would have averaged a C-, but he wasn't really a trouble maker in class. He did try his best, but academia was not a strong point. Nevertheless, he still completed all set work from all his teachers, which was more than could be said for a lot of students. It is true that he had run-ins with some teachers, as the majority of students tend to face in their school life, simply because some personalities are always going to clash. From my observation, in Glen's case, much of it was generated by teachers who saw an opportunity to square the ledger for Allan's indiscretions. Most teachers grew to like Glen after realising he was not the monster that some painted him to be.

"The major issue for Glen at school was to prove that he could rise above his station in life. His nickname was 'cement-head' due to his brother working at Cockburn Cement. He was also burdened with Allan's reputation, so he set out to prove that he was different; that he was a decent person and thus restore credibility to the family name. This was on-going throughout his school life. In particular, he wanted to prove wrong those teachers who yelled 'You'll never make anything of yourself Jakovich'.

Football was the vehicle which allowed him to prove his point. Glen is the best schoolboy footballer I've seen and I've had a bit to do with some talented kids, coaching Quit Cup for nearly 15 years. Glen was a natural who took on the older kids and, more often than not, won. As he entered Year 10, he really started to dominate. He already had it in his mind to have a go at South Fremantle the following year and he had the confidence of youth that he could succeed at such a young age.

"I was at his debut game for South Fremantle at Leederville Oval in 1989 and, from memory, he started on the bench and then went to centre half-forward. He had a reasonable first-up game, but this was a triumph bigger than simply making a debut as a 16-year-old. Glen's father had passed away in February and he had become the man of the household, plus he had to keep it together to achieve his aim of playing league football. It is his biggest regret – and also his greatest driving force – that his father never saw him play at the highest level, whether that be WAFL or AFL. Each game for Glen is, in many ways, a tribute to his Dad who gave him the values and integrity that he still holds dear today.

"School life was difficult for Glen and he faced more hardships than the average kid. The family was not wealthy and all they had came from sweat and hard toil. Glen loved the sporting competitions he had with his brothers, whether that be footy or cricket, but he cherished fishing with his Dad most of all. It brought father and son closer together. Darko often related stories about life 'back in the old country', involving family gatherings that revolved around fishing, cooking, drinking wine and the family gathering together to sing songs.

"There was also the dark side, in particular the horrors that all Slavic people endured during World War II. From those conversations, Glen developed an affinity for his father's homeland and an appreciation of what love of country and family actually meant. Thus, for him, it was natural to assist the family in the garden. Picking carrots and onions before and after school was not only assisting, but also playing a part in the family unit – this became more pronounced when Darko was diagnosed with cancer. School became a 'secondary concern' as the garden and Darko's illness took hold. At school, Glen didn't let things get to him but, rather stoically, continued to perform the best he could.

"His sense of loyalty that is often exhibited to family was also extended to Hamilton High School and it manifested itself through sporting competitions, and not just football. Glen was a fierce competitor in athletics and represented Hamilton High in field events every year. He was determined to do his bit and help 'Hammy' get over the line. This typified his high school years – not the best student, but still the one to get the best out of himself, for both the school and the individual."

Tony Granich

Stepping up to the mark

Pushing into the seniors

FROM Glen Jakovich's stellar days in junior football spawned a wonderful senior career, the first indication of what lay ahead coming in 1989. Jakovich was asked to train with the South Fremantle colts squad, but he had other ideas and turned up for the start of senior training unannounced.

"The 1989 season was my biggest in terms of improvement as a developing player," Jakovich said. "South Fremantle would send out letters to everyone in the district inviting them to play with the colts and, at the end of 1988, I had the standard letter. But I didn't get an invitation to train with the league side; they thought I was too young at 15 and not turning 16 until March. So I just rocked up to league training and, when they went through the roll, my name wasn't there. They knew who I was because I'd been playing in the colts, but the team manager went over and asked Stan Magro and Tony Micale, who was the assistant coach at the time, whether I could train. They said I was too young and should be training with the colts. But I virtually demanded that I should train one session with the league. Santo Pasqua was the team manager and he was a bit anxious about it, but I suppose he could see the determination on my face.

"There was a bit of a kerfuffle about it, which I didn't like. With 50 or 60 blokes waiting to start pre-season training, I wasn't that keen on making any fuss. In the end they said okay and I guess they expected me to fall out after the first couple of laps of a 4km time trial. Stan has spoken to me about it a few times since – they didn't think I'd be able to go the distance. They thought they'd just send me back to the colts with no harm done, but I came second in the 4km time trial. I was leading all the way and just got over-run by Damien Leebeck... I don't think the coaches could believe how distraught I was at losing the time trial. I think that might have flicked a light on in Stan's head. He must have thought 'here's a kid on the first night of pre-season training, we've got 60 guys and he's spewing that he's only run second in a time trial.'

"I knew they would cut 20 before Christmas and it was important to make an impression. The regular league blokes were there... the Matera brothers, Maurice Rioli, the Wilson boys from Mandurah. Richard Geary, Mark Bayliss, who had gone to Collingwood the year before. There were a lot of established players as well as the add-ons who come down after being invited. Maurice didn't run because he was in the twilight of his career, but it was such an honour to be at training with him. Four months later, I was playing in the first game of the season with him. I really trained the house down so, when it came to scratch matches, they couldn't leave me out because my training form had been so good. The next time there was a 4km time trial I knew I wouldn't get over-run because I had gone out of the blocks too early the first time. This time, I held a bit back in reserve, I was fit and pretty strong for a young fella.

"Because I would finish school at 3pm I'd catch the bus to Freo Oval and that meant I had two hours before training, so I'd go to the gym and start my own weights programme. That's probably not ideal in today's footy, but I felt it would help develop my physical presence. Big guys like Craig Edwards were there at the time and I knew I'd be getting belted around by all these blokes. The first intra-club practice match, I played in the back pocket and went all right and from there I got better and better and was just surprising everyone.

"My skills were okay and I had confidence in my ability. The key was to show them how determined I was – not that I was this silky skilled young bloke who could kick a goal and take a mark over the top of a pack. That wasn't my objective. I wanted to show them that I'd work my butt off and felt that, by doing the hard work, the rest would look after itself. I knew I was good enough to play and had the skills to succeed.

"At that time it was difficult because the old man was sick and I had to weigh up all these things – South were going through a bit of a rough time financially as well. The club had

Champions are not solely depicted by their on-field exploits. Long-serving South Fremantle administrator Brian Ciccotosto regards Glen Jakovich in the highest bracket of players to ever represent the Bulldogs. Perhaps the biggest compliment any South player could be afforded would be to draw a comparison with the club's greatest player, Stephen Michael.

"When Glen Jakovich came down to South he wanted to be treated as a man, even though he was just a kid," says Ciccotosto. "We had a busy bee about 1989 because the club was broke and we needed to spruce the ground up a bit. A mate of mine brought his lawnmower along, so he and I started work on the bank near the scoreboard. The grass was about a metre high and next thing Jako walks over and says 'do you guys want a hand.' I thought, well he's been pulling onions all his life, and welcomed his offer. He pitched in and just kept at it until the job was done. I can't ever recall another player doing something like that.

"I regard Jako in the Stephen Michael class. Michael was probably a better player, I regard him as the best I've seen, but Jako is right up there with him. Blokes like Jako and Stephen always put in off the field as well. When Jako played his 250th game for the Eagles I wrote to him and said I regarded him in the same esteem in which I hold Stephen Michael.

"Stephen epitomised what the champions are all about. He's generous, committed and is always back for Hughes Medal (fairest and best) counts. If I have a special request, he'll always oblige. When Jako retires he will not only be remembered as a great footballer, he will be remembered for all the other things as well. He and blokes like John Worsfold and Peter Sumich have always been very strong South Fremantle people, even though they have played relatively few games for us.

"In 1988 Jako played 15 games of colts and the next year he was in the league side. In his first year at the Eagles, 1990, he played just 10 games at South and Brad Collard beat him for the fairest and best by just one vote. If he had played another game he would have won. Before he was called up to the Eagles, he was so far in front he was lonely.

"When he first started in the senior team, I said to Stan Magro, the coach at the time, to start him in the forward pocket because he loved kicking a goal. Mind you, he didn't enjoy a goal as much as his brother, Allan. I can remember when I was coaching the colts and Allan was playing, I told him one night at training he wasn't allowed to kick the ball. He could run with it, he could bounce it and he could hand pass it, but he couldn't kick it. Then I played him as a ruck-rover and he still kicked eight goals! But Glen Jakovich was a bit like Tom Grljusich, he could play in any of the key positions.

"The year Glen played three levels of State football, I said to him 'why would you want to play Teal Cup when you've already done that?' He said he didn't want to miss any level and that he wanted to play footy with his mates."

Brian Ciccotosto

been run down and there were certain issues going on around the place. They had a couple of busy bees where the players came down and Stan Magro, who was a painter by trade, organised all these paints from Dulux. We stripped all the change rooms down, and the social hall, and re-painted it all over one weekend and had a barbecue down at the club. Weeds had grown up through the concrete paving and everyone was helping out as part of a SOS (Save Our South) because the club was about $1 million in debt.

"Bill Hughes was the president, his sister was Eileen Bond (wife of Alan Bond at the time) and she donated $25,000 for the paint and also some new pictures and restored old team photographs and things from the early days of the club's history. It really got the club back up and it was a good place to be. Here was a club that was struggling, on the back of a first semi final defeat when Suma (Peter Sumich), Mark Sambrailo and all those guys were playing. They kicked 1.11 against East Fremantle in the first quarter and really should have won. They won their last eight to qualify for the finals.

"I couldn't go to one of the busy bees because I had to look after the old man as Mum was working and he was pretty much bedridden at the time. It was tough because I had to give Dad morphine injections because he was in so much pain. Someone had to look after him and I was the only one home. I kept it pretty quiet, I didn't want too many people knowing about it, but when I couldn't attend the club function some officials became aware of it and were pretty good about it. The old man died on February 19, 1989 and I took a week off school, but I didn't take any time off footy.

When Darko Jakovich was diagnosed with cancer, the two eldest boys had left home, so much of the responsibility of looking after him and comforting Mary fell with Glen. Tragically, history repeated itself when Darko passed away when Glen was 15; Darko had lost his Dad when he was 15, so he stayed at home and looked after his Mum and his young brother who was still at school.

"Glen was pretty good when his Dad passed away," Mary said. "I was able to talk to him about it, but Gary couldn't talk about his Dad at the time. He can now, but he couldn't then. Glen used to go to the Dalmatinac Club with his Dad where they played bowls; he did those sorts of things with his father. Glen loved that club and used to go every Sunday. He still goes there with his wife.

"When his Dad got cancer, we just let everything go in the garden because I had to concentrate on my husband, take him backwards and forwards to hospital; when he died, Glen got the crop out. He got his relatives and his mates to help him out and got a bit of money for it. Glen was unreal at that age. I live on seven acres of land, the yard is big and he used to say to me 'Mum, you look after the inside and I will look after the outside.' When he started playing for the Eagles he used to pinch my bills and pay them. Then he would say 'you buy the food, I will pay the bills.'"

Mary Jakovich

"Stan was pretty good, but it was a tough time. When I first went down to South my brother Allan had left the club on uneasy terms and probably wasted his time a bit at South as he got caught up with a crowd that were yahooing. That was Allan's nature and he was dropped from the league side a couple of times for undisciplined acts. When I came through it was perceived that I had a bit of that in me as well."

That perception, which also hovered over Jakovich's head at school, proved totally misplaced and, in stark contrast, the younger of the Jakovich clan was absolutely committed to make a success of his football. He was a big kid, physically, but had been forced to grow up in a hurry, in every sense, as he endured a period in his life; this impacted tremendously on him. To say it was a tough personal period simply does not emphasise the difficulty.

"In that time I grew from an immature 14-year-old kid into a mature 15-year-old young man," he said. "My school wasn't a priority, the family was deeply in debt and we had to borrow money to pay for Dad's funeral and head stone... it was all quite hard. It was just Mum and me at home at the time. Gary was working away and Allan was playing footy in Darwin, so I had the responsibility of the garden as well as school, which was the last thing on my list of priorities. I didn't like school at all.

"The only thing I felt good about was playing footy. Mum and I just worked hard to pay off our debts and I was getting $125 a league game so my footy money went towards our survival. I was in Year 11 and playing league footy – for me that was fantastic. I felt that a few teachers resented me at the time because I wasn't putting a lot of energy into my schooling. I was marking time at school.

"You got a lot of attention from the other kids and I suppose the teachers thought I was a bit big-headed. I played my first league game the week after I turned 16 – playing league football for South Fremantle in that district at the time was quite a big deal. As far as I was

"Glen never liked school. The headmaster used to growl at him, saying 'football's not going to get you anywhere.' But football was all he wanted and it did get him somewhere, didn't it? When he couldn't kick the ball outside, he used to stand inside the house at one door way and kick it around the corner into the next one.

"I was hoping he would do well, but I wasn't sure of it. Because of the way he played his junior football, I thought there was a good chance he would be successful, but I never really knew how it would pan out for him."

Mary Jakovich

concerned, I had found my career and to boot with the rest of it. I knew I couldn't keep going to school either, but I just wanted to get through my first year of league footy and see how I went.

"I played every game bar two, when I went to Melbourne for the Teal Cup, and after that we won the second semi and went straight into a grand final against Claremont. I played against Tony Evans, Ryan Turnbull, Gerard Neesham and Ben Allan, who won the Simpson Medal. That was the biggest year of my life and was the foundation of where I am today. When I look back at the whole year, it was fantastic, but it was also difficult for me on and off field. Actually, it was relatively easy on the footy field.

From as early as he can remember, Glen Jakovich knew what he wanted to do with his life and he was not prepared to compromise in his quest to achieve that goal. South Fremantle stalwart Brian Ciccotosto, an outstanding rover before assuming the role of development officer and then general manager of the Bulldogs, remembers a young Jakovich wandering into his office and asking whether he could use the club gymnasium.

"I asked him how old he was and he said 14," Ciccotosto recalls. "I was thinking, having worked with blokes like Brian Douge (former Hawthorn and Subiaco ruck-rover and an expert in the area of physical fitness), that you can't start kids on weights too young. But I thought Jacko had probably been picking onions from the age of five or six, so I didn't think it would do him any harm. He was never a skinny boy, but obviously he has bulked up since joining the Eagles. He was the youngest by far using the gym. I took a liking to him and knew he would do the work. He loved South Fremantle and we took a strong interest in the Jakovich family because his brothers were playing for us at the time."

That trip to the Bulldogs bunker was the first of many as he strived to carve out a WAFL career with the hope that it would be a stepping stone to bigger things.

"Glen came into my office another day and saw this South Fremantle plaque sitting on the wall and said he wanted it," Ciccotosto said. "I told him that when he played his first league game for South Fremantle, it was his. The trouble was that I got rid of the plaque before he played a game! I chased all over the place trying to track one down. We had them made in Korea or somewhere and I couldn't find one anywhere."

Brian Ciccotosto

"I played with Willie Rioli and Greg Turner, who were young players touted as having big futures. Playing with Maurice made me hungry to play because I'd been a seven-year-old going down to Fremantle Oval and watching him play and eight years later I'm playing in the same team. It was great to play alongside someone who had carved out such an illustrious career. I just remember saying to myself that I wouldn't waste the opportunity to play with such a great player. I had a fantastic year, I think I came second in the goal-kicking playing at full-forward and centre half-forward.

"At the end of the year, I sat down with the club and asked if they could help me find a job in Fremantle because I didn't want to go to school any more. I was wasting my time at school. Brian Ciccotosto lined up a job as an apprentice mechanic with Backshall Ford, who was a major sponsor at the time. It was a trial period of six months and I got through that okay. I had grown up in the market garden and we had learned to fix things ourselves, so I enjoyed the job. It was another source of income as well, which helped pay the bills at home.

"We leased the market garden out to my uncle Bob and, all of a sudden, Mum and I turned things around and paid off our debts. I guess at that stage of life I was very different to most 16 and 17-year-olds because I'd made a commitment to play league footy and part of that was not to do some of the things that your average teenager did at that age."

Football clubs are often an education for a young man and, for Glen Jakovich, part of his 'development' came after a game in Kalgoorlie, playing for South Fremantle against Subiaco as a 16-year-old.

"The only time I went out was with the footy team," Jakovich recalls. "Stan Magro was big on that for team morale. My third league game was against Subiaco in Kalgoorlie and, after the match, we had about an hour to kill. The traditional thing was to go down to Hay Street and, being the young bloke and not knowing a lot about me, because they had never seen me drink, they threw some cash into a hat and wanted to pay for an experience for me. We walked in and I remember seeing one of the most glamourous women, well she was at the time, and she came up to me. I panicked and said no. All the boys looked down on me for not taking up the offer and they all volunteered to take up the opportunity. I just didn't think that was the right thing for a professional footballer."

Glen Jakovich

From good stock

Father's influence

IN GLEN Jakovich's formative years, the relationship with his father Darko was exceptional. The bond between many fathers and sons is strong, but none could have been stronger than that of Jako and his dad, so you can imagine how difficult it was to deal with his father's deterioration in health.

"When Dad died, we still had a crop in so I had to get it out," Jakovich said, matter of factly. "A few of my cousins came over and helped out and we went to the market, got whatever we could and paid off the expenses. We were running in the red, and Mum took more hours at work. We had a few family people who pretty quickly came to our aid. Mum was born here, but her parents were from the same island as my father.

"For me it was tough. The old man got crook in November and only lasted three months after the diagnosis of cancer. He was crook a little before that, but he wasn't diagnosed until November. To start with, he just thought he had a bug, some sort of virus, but he had skeletal cancer. It was right through his bones. He had no hope.

"He stayed at home and was bed-ridden and needed shots of morphine five or six times a day just to get up and go to the toilet. He was sent home from hospital to at least be in his own surroundings. It was a very difficult time, but I was prepared for it straight away. We knew he wasn't going to survive.

"Mum told me one day after school that he had cancer and, at the time, I couldn't accept it. I didn't want to accept it. We were very close because I was the youngest and the other two guys were living their own lives. Gary was 26, Allan was 21 and they were young men. I was a kid. I saw more of it but, from that point of view, I believe it made me the person I am today.

"Both Gary and Allan played league footy for South and Dad watched them play. My biggest regret is that, after almost 350 games all up – State of Origin, premierships and all, my Dad didn't see one game. What motivates me, still today, is that I believe he's up in the clouds looking down and I feel an obligation to perform well because he's watching. The hard task master that he was, I reckon he would be pretty proud. I used to visit his grave before every game when I first started with the Eagles. I don't do that as much any more because your life changes, I have my own family. But I will never forget him. I feel his spirit is with me. I have had footy role models like Maurice Rioli, but my father was my role model for life.

"I have learned more about him in the years since he passed away than the time he was with us because I was too young to really know him before he died. Finding out more about him has made me appreciate the hurdles he faced in life. He came to this country and couldn't speak the language and had no education or qualifications. He went up north to Carnarvon because a lot of the Croatian migrants went there and share farmed to get a bit of money behind them to buy their own land. That is basically what he did. He was probably up there for five years before coming down to Perth.

"Whenever life gets hard for me, or I have to deal with adversity, I think back to my time as a 15-year-old, having to inject my father with morphine to help him manage his pain. Learning how they lived in the former Yugoslavia under communism and how they struggled was important for me. They had it pretty hard, but they appreciated what they had. The simple things in life."

"I didn't see him play a lot in the State Schoolboys or Teal Cup because I was in Adelaide, but I played against him when I represented South Australia and he played for the WAFL. It was at Football Park and he was just 17. Mum came over for the game and it wasn't that long after dad had passed away.

"I think I kicked something like 4.8 or 5.8 that day and Glen actually played on me for a while. I kicked a couple on him just before three-quarter time and I can remember walking alongside him on the way to the huddle. He had the double mouth guard because he had braces on his bottom teeth and I remember him blowing like a cow.

"I had just started to get a feel for the conditions, because Footy Park often had a bit of a flukey breeze blowing through. At the start of the last quarter he lined up on me again, but a quick change was made. I don't know whether he hadn't looked at the white board during the break, but he didn't play on me again that day."

Allan Jakovich

The Croatian background

KNOWING where he came from has helped Glen Jakovich understand who he is. And that has meant re-tracing his roots back to the Croatian island where his father was born and to which his mother also had strong links. Jakovich has since been a regular visitor to his father's homeland and it holds a special place in his heart.

"I have been back to Croatia four times, just to see where he lived, how he lived, the school he went to," Jakovich reflected. "That was an eye-opener because it's a very old country. Under communism it was pretty basic living. Then there was the civil war which led to the collapse of Yugoslavia. I had been there in 1976 with Mum and Dad and had all these spot memories, but I had no real recollection of the place. That's why I went back after the war. Growing up, I always heard about where Mum and Dad had come from and I thought I had to get back there and find out about their roots.

"I went back in 1998 after we'd been to Barcelona on a footy trip and Croatia was just around the corner, so I went back and I've been back every two years since. It was a very emotional time but, as I was sitting on a ferry going to the island where my parents came from, I just felt I knew where I was going. I flew into Split, where my uncle met me at the airport. We had dinner that night and caught a ferry the next morning to the island which was my father's home. It's amazing because 100 percent of me comes from that island, my Mum's parents were born there, my father was born there.

"The island is Solta, about half an hour from Split, right on the Mediterranean coast. It's a beautiful place, especially in summer. The country has evolved a little through tourism, but it is a very, very old country. The war in Bosnia was officially over when I went back in 1998, but there was still a lot of sniping going on. The war in Kosovo was heating up between the Albanians and the Serbs. I remember getting into Zagreb Airport and heaps of peace keeping troops were boarding my flight – Czechs, Slovenians, Belgians – all army personnel going in to do what they needed to do. I had a pretty good understanding of the war; I'd followed it pretty closely.

"Yugoslavia consisted of six States with three different religions – Catholics, Muslims and Orthodox – all with different dialects and languages. They were different people living under the banner of Yugoslavia, which for some years worked and for some years didn't. In the end it erupted into war... it was tragic that it happened because so many innocent lives were lost. I'm not here to say who is right or wrong because I really don't know, but in the end no-one wins from that situation.

"When I went back, it was sad to see so many buildings shelled and bombed, even our island copped a few shells. Houses had caved in after being hit by mortar. I have a few cousins over there. I like to keep in touch with what is happening. I have a passion for the country; they have a very simple way of life and I like to see the country prospering.

"They have had some significant happenings since then, they came third in the World Cup in soccer in their first ever campaign. Goran Ivanisevic, who I met at the Hopman Cup in Perth one year, won the Wimbledon tennis title and they have had a couple of Olympic gold medallists. Hopefully, the country is changing for the better and it seems things are getting better all the time. It's going to take a long time, but the process has started.

"I learned to speak Croatian because Dad couldn't speak English when he first arrived. There was also a community club called Spearwood Dalmatinac and all the ethnics used to go there every Sunday. They would play soccer, bocce and cards. We used to hang around there as kids and all my cousins were there as well so we spoke Croatian. I don't read it as well as I can speak it, but I can pick up the key words. I'm very proud of my heritage.

"Emely went there with her sister and her grandparents before the war. She is from an island called Korcula where Marco Polo was born. I have taken photos of his house."

Eagle bound

That footy treble

THROUGH the course of his career, Glen Jakovich has created some special pieces of history – four club champion awards, All-Australian selection, club games-played record and the first West Coast player to earn AFL life membership after playing 300 games. But one of his finest achievements came before his West Coast career had even begun.

In 1990, Jakovich achieved the rare distinction of representing his State at three levels in the same season – he played Teal Cup (the national 18s carnival), then made the WAFL State side and soon after was the only WAFL club player included in WA's State of Origin team. That achievement is unlikely to ever occur again.

"I knew at the time it was something pretty unique, but it was a strange feeling," Jakovich said. "Here I was in my second year of footy and playing with the likes of Steve Malaxos, Mark Bairstow, Michael Mitchell, John Ironmonger, Darren Bewick, Peter Wilson, Earl Spalding blokes like that... To play with those blokes was quite an experience after playing Teal Cup and for the WAFL team.

"I played another full year at South and that laid the foundation for getting drafted. It was an important part of my development to play in those games. It didn't bother me at the time who drafted me, I just wanted to get drafted by an AFL club. If I'd gone to St Kilda or one of the great clubs of the time, Hawthorn, Essendon or Carlton, it didn't bother me. I just wanted an opportunity. No other clubs spoke to me. It was different back then because the Eagles had priority selections of players aged between 16 and 19, so the other clubs didn't speak to me, probably because they figured they couldn't get me.

"But I don't think Mick liked the way I played. The culture I grew up in, I didn't do a lot of the team things. Because I dominated as a junior, I tried to carry that dominance through to WAFL level. It worked for me, but at times I was criticised for not doing the team things. I accepted that, it was just a learning thing and probably I just needed to be drilled about it a little more. It was hard because it had been in my game from when I first started. I would go and get the ball, kick it, mark it and basically doing everything I wanted to do individually, but in a team structure.

"Allan played his footy that way too. He was the hungriest player ever. They laugh at me when I'm outside 50 trying to kick a goal; he'd be on the half-back flank and would have a shot! There's nothing wrong with that, but hopefully I've altered things. Sometimes I revert back to that style to try and play some good footy or to lift the team. In junior teams I was always looked upon as the bloke who would do that and I felt like I had that responsibility. When you do that for the first 10 or 12 years of your football life, it's hard to change it. Mick and I didn't get on all that well to start with because I don't think he agreed with the way I played."

So unconvinced by Jakovich's self-centred style of football was Malthouse that he took some persuading to actually secure the precocious teenager as one of two zone selections from WA at the end of 1990.

"I reckon Mick Moylan and Trevor Nisbett convinced him that they should draft me," Jakovich said. "I remember my first emotion when getting drafted was one of relief. Mick Moylan rang me at Backshall Ford to tell me. Unfortunately, as a 17-year-old at the time, I had received a fair bit of publicity, but there was this negativity that I might not get drafted. The media was asking who would the Eagles select with their priority choices. The year before they got Peter Mann and Ryan Turnbull, so who would they take this year?

"There was a bit of publicity about it and they had certainly pencilled in Mitchell White – I gather Mick was really rapt in him. But who was going to get the other spot? They had three or four blokes in the mix and my name was one of them. I was worried after being built up to be this next big whatever because I had played State of Origin, WA footy and Teal Cup all in the same year and I'd had a pretty good WAFL season. I thought I'd been set up for the great big fall. When Mick Moylan rang me, I was just so relieved. I wasn't excited, just relieved.

"I rang Mum straight away because she was working at the South Fremantle shopping complex. I can remember Chris Young coming down from Channel 7 and interviewing me."

Getting drafted was just the first stage of the plan. It seemed Malthouse, in particular, required further convincing that this exceptional young athlete could fit into his game plan. Malthouse knew the kid could play, he just wasn't sure that he could adjust to West Coast's team-oriented method.

It's a fine line between being good enough as a youth to be noticed in the embryonic stages of your football career and being so good and so big as to dominate right the way through. When the West Coast Eagles were assessing the claims of potential choices as zonal selections ahead of the 1990 national draft, Glen Jakovich's opportunity was not a fait accompli. For a young man who had played Teal Cup, represented WA at WAFL level and then earned All-Australian honours in the same year, he might have considered himself a shoo-in for a place on the Eagles list. But the fact he had dominated junior football and been allowed to play his own game for so long, could have worked against him.

Unlike the process involved in the draft in this era of the game, incoming West Coast coach Mick Malthouse had not met Jakovich when he and the club's recruiting staff discussed the issue; however, he had watched Jakovich closely, had seen him dictate terms with the WA Teal Cup team and was also in sparkling touch with South Fremantle. The questions did not concentrate on his ability to play the game, but more the capacity to develop further and play a role in a team where the structure was based around the whole unit rather than the individual.

"Initially I was worried about Glen's discipline, he was so well developed physically that he was already a man and I wondered how he would mature," Malthouse said. "I hadn't met him at that stage either, although the recruiting people obviously had. These days players are very closely scrutinised, but back then I didn't speak to him. I had watched him play State of Origin footy and also watched him play for South Fremantle. He played at centre half-back at times, but didn't seem to take a lot of notice of his opponents. He managed to get a lot of the ball, but so did his opponent. I wondered whether South Fremantle was the best club for him because he seemed to have carte blanche to do what he liked.

"We looked at a number of players and assessed what each of them could do, how they would develop and what they offered. As it turned out, those doubts I had over Glen were erased in the first month. You wouldn't find a player who was easier to coach. He was willing to do everything he could to improve as a player and was ready to listen to what he was told.

"Some of our initial concerns probably came about because he was such a big kid and had played the game pretty much on his own terms in junior football. But when you play State of Origin football you are against the best in the country and for such a young man he did a pretty good job in that game. Southern Europeans, in Glen's case Croatians, tend to mature very early. By the time they are 15 or 16 they are often the shape of a man. Someone like Jason Ball, who was still built like a stick at 19 or 20, didn't mature physically until he was 23 or 24, so Glen was five or six years ahead of him in terms of his physical development. I knew Glen could play. He had played Teal Cup, State football and State of Origin all in the same year so there was no doubt he had plenty of ability. And he soon showed that he had a great work ethic to go with that ability."

Mick Malthouse

"When I went to Eagles pre-season in 1991 I had the same approach that I'd had at South Fremantle a couple of years earlier," Jakovich recounted. "That was to win all the beach runs and to train the house down. I was up with Dean Kemp and Peter Matera in the early beach runs because I had to be noticed. There was a squad of 52 and only 20 positions in the team. I had to get a spot in the 20.

"I had the same pre-meditated plan for the pre-season runs and that was to win them all. At school in Years 8, 9 and 10, I was the champion boy and then, when the Year 11 and 12s were combined, I was the first Year 11 to win Upper School champion. I used to win the 400, 800, 1500, high jump and long jump. The first year with the Eagles was a matter of proving to people that I deserved to be where I was."

When that pre-season was winding down and the focus turned to the rapidly-approaching qualifying rounds, Malthouse asked his young charge how he expected his first season in the AFL to unfold.

"When Mick asked what my goals were, I wrote them down for him," Jakovich said. "He came back and said my goals were set way above what I could achieve. I sensed he was going to say that, just looking at his body language. I pencilled in that I wanted to play 12 or 13 league games, I wanted to play State of Origin again and there were a few other individual things in there which I don't think he liked. I wanted to set some individual landmarks so that when I got there I would feel as though I was contributing to the team. I needed to do that to be a team player, even though they were individual goals.

"Mick came back and said I would be lucky to play two or three games, so I re-assessed and put down 7-10 games. I thought I'd meet him somewhere near half-way. I played 16 games in my first year, four finals and a grand final and won rookie of the year."

If Malthouse doubted in the pre-season that Jakovich had the attributes required to succeed at the highest level, he certainly didn't show those reservations when his young charge eventually forced his way into the team. The raw teenage talent was pitted against some of the game's luminaries.

"Stephen Kernahan was my opponent in only my third league game," Jakovich recalled. "It was the first game the Eagles lost that year against Carlton at Princes Park. We lost by three points. That was the day the fans ran onto the ground, they had a go at Karl Langdon and one bloke punched Dwayne Lamb from behind. It was also the year we won 12 straight.

"In my first league game, I played up forward and on and off the bench, Suma had done his hammy the week before and that was my spot. We were sitting on the plane and Mick said 'you played well, kicked a couple of goals, you did everything we asked of you, but Suma is coming back next week, so I will have to shuffle it up.' I knew then, though, that he wasn't going to drop me. One of the assets I have as a person is an ability to read what people are feeling and thinking and, through Mick's body language, I felt he didn't want to drop me. I reckon he could see that I'd worked so hard to get there and he knew I was going to produce some good footy and to drop me was going to be pretty hard. He didn't drop me, even though Suma came back the next week and kicked 13 goals against Footscray. I had to play on Glen Coleman, who was their centre half-forward and I played four good quarters at centre half-back.

"In those days you had to ring in on a Thursday to find out if you were playing. I rang Mick and he said he was going to play me and I suppose he could hear my excitement on the phone. He said 'can you do the job?' and I remember saying f.... oath. I apologised for swearing and he said, 'you'll be right'.

"I played pretty well but, late in the last quarter, I flew for a mark four deep. I took it, but it was against his rules. I won an award that night, but Mick drilled me for that. He wanted to have a crack at me and I could sense it. Every time I slipped up, for the faintest little thing, he would really get into me. Then he said 'I don't know whether I can trust you playing on Stephen Kernahan next week if you're going to fly from four deep and try to mark. You won't mark it every time at this level from four deep.' That was when I knew I would play the following week, he had me earmarked for Kernahan. I went okay on Kernahan and then played against St Kilda in front of a record crowd at the time and did a job on Stewart Loewe.

"I really put a lot into my first four weeks. Game three on Kernahan, I felt like I was playing for survival and that, if he kicked five or six, I would be back at South. But here I was, against the best player in the competition, and there was just no way I was going to let him have it on his own terms. I couldn't afford to compromise and had this no-failure attitude.

"I don't think I won Mick over until half-way through the 1992 season. Suma and Woosha, who were pretty close to Mick, took him fishing during the off-season after 1991 and Mick told them he still wasn't sure about me. I only found that out recently.

"That was after 16 games and four finals. I had played pretty well in some big games, but I needed to convince those people that I wasn't going to be a one-year wonder. I took the same approach that I had at South Fremantle after a good first year. At South I had to convince Stan Magro, Cicco and Terry Dean (now club president) that I wasn't going to be a one-year wonder and in my second year I played State of Origin footy. The same thing with the Eagles, when I was earmarked for 2-3 games, I ended up playing 16.

"Then, 1992, well that speaks for itself. I was third in the club champion award in a premiership year. I finally won Mick over. I didn't get the second year blues, but I had been prepared for that because I'd faced them playing for South Fremantle. I felt that grounding was pretty important."

By the time the 1990 AFL Draft came around, everyone had heard of Glen Jakovich. So influential had he been in his junior career, that his name was one of the hottest in football.

Given the West Coast Eagles had two priority selections and Jakovich was an outstanding young West Australian, it seemed a fait accompli that he would play for the local club. But, as the draft drew closer, there was some conjecture that Jakovich might be overlooked.

Current West Coast Eagles chief executive Trevor Nisbett was the football manager back then and, while he concedes Jakovich was one of several players under consideration, he says there was never any real risk of the club over-looking the powerful young South Fremantle prodigy. It was more a case of analysing all the other talent available and also to send a message to the rising star that nothing should be taken for granted.

"He was in the wash-up with three or four other guys the club was looking at," Nisbett said. "It was fair to suggest Mick (Malthouse) was concerned about his pace, or lack of it, but I don't think there were any deep-seated concerns that we weren't going to select him.

"It was a matter of trying to lower Glen's expectations as much as saying there were other guys who could be selected ahead of him, which was never going to be the case. There were enough people who had seen him play and wanted him on the list because he had indicated he would be a very good player. And that's exactly how it turned out.

"There was no doubt he was going to be selected as one of the two players (Mitchell White was well up in our thoughts). There were probably two or three others we had considered to that point. Glen had played forward until mid-way through that season when Stan Magro, who was coaching South Fremantle, played him at centre half-back. I had been in contact with Stan and he thought that was where he would play. While he could play at either end, Stan thought Glen could be a sensational centre half-back."

Trevor Nisbett

Meeting destiny

LONG BEFORE he was drafted by the West Coast Eagles as a compensatory choice from the club's West Australian 'zone', Glen Jakovich was certain that it was his life's destiny to play elite football.

Up to that point, almost everything in his life was driven by his desire to succeed in his chosen field. When he was drafted, along with Subiaco half-forward Mitchell White as a zonal selection in the 1990 ballot, Jakovich was already a familiar name in football circles – and not just because of the exploits of older brother, Allan. Five years Glen's senior, Allan was a member of the famous 1985 Teal Cup side, a fabulous combination which was the first to claim the national under-17 title for WA. Among Allan's teammates in that wonderful team were players of the calibre of John Worsfold, Peter Sumich, Chris Lewis, Chris Waterman, Paul Peos, Guy McKenna and Scott Watters – all destined to be teammates of Glen.

Allan, a freakish forward with an amazing goal sense, had moved to Adelaide and would later advance to play senior football with Melbourne, while Glen, the youngest of three brothers, was carving out an amazing record in junior ranks. He played State schoolboys (under 16s) and Teal Cup (under 17s) for two years and in 1990 he completed the amazing treble – playing Teal Cup, representing the WAFL at interstate level (playing against his brother for the first, but not the last, time) against South Australia at Football Park, and then earning selection in the WA State of Origin team. Never before had a young footballer achieved so much in the embryonic stages of his career.

When Jakovich arrived at West Coast, he was determined to play senior level football. Others, at 17 years of age, might have considered themselves development players on an AFL list, taking a long-term view to their career. Not Jakovich. If he was on a list, he was there to play. He was not there to make up the numbers.

Those within the inner sanctum at West Coast recognised Jakovich's precocious talent, but took the view that his enthusiasm needed to be tempered. So, despite eye-catching form with South Fremantle, he was forced to wait until Round 11 for his chance after White and Ashley McIntosh, a father-son selection in the 1989 draft, were preferred when key position vacancies were created through injury.

"In 1991 we won the first 12 games and, when I look back on it now, it was quite an extraordinary time when I went into the team," recalls Jakovich. "Mick Malthouse said at the start of the year that it was going to be tough for me to break into the side because he obviously thought the team would have a good season on the back of the finals series they had enjoyed in 1990. But I was determined to force my way into the team and do everything possible to ensure I got the chance. My training, my fitness and everything else was geared towards getting a chance.

"I got off to a crackerjack start at South Fremantle. My form was as good as it had ever been and I really enjoyed my time at South and was passionate about playing for the club, but my real objective was to play with the West Coast Eagles. When I went back to South, it was a means of getting a chance of playing with the Eagles. I enjoyed the culture of South Fremantle, I was their player, but then I wasn't. I was contracted to the West Coast Eagles, but I was playing with South. I never trained with South, I just went there on the weekends. But I felt like I was a winner either way because I enjoyed my football playing with both clubs. If it didn't work out with the Eagles, I would spend 12 or 13 years with South Fremantle and that wasn't a bad fall-back position."

With that positive attitude, Jakovich flourished at South Fremantle and his WAFL form attracted support, at least outside the club.

"At the time I was getting publicity because of my form in the WAFL, kicking five or six goals from centre half-forward," Jakovich recalled. "The media was putting the question to the match committee about when I was going to get a chance. Then they played Mitchell White ahead of me. There was a late withdrawal before the Essendon game in Round 7 and Mitch made his league debut, so he was the first out of the three of us – myself and Ashley McIntosh being the other two – to get an opportunity.

"Then another chance opened up, I had kicked six goals the week before and everyone considered me a certainty to play. Milli (McIntosh) hadn't played a lot of WAFL footy, but he got the nod. I was disappointed, but I had a steely resolve to play sooner or later because I was hell-bent on continuing to play well at South Fremantle.

"I then kicked three goals in the Foundation Day Derby and won the Clive Lewington Medal as best-afield. I'd gone to Melbourne as the emergency for the game against Richmond and Ashley played pretty well, kicking a couple of goals and I thought, well I'll go home and play in a Derby, so it was a pretty good second option. So I went back and did that. Suma did his hamstring against Richmond and I knew after playing well for South that I would get my chance. So I went to Carrara and played against the Brisbane Bears.

"Although I had wanted to play six weeks earlier, there were no sour grapes because I knew they had done it to see how I could handle it mentally and see how I coped with the disappointment."

After being elevated for that Brisbane game, Jakovich would never play for South Fremantle again. Remarkably, he had polled so heavily in the first nine games with the Bulldogs that he finished runner-up in the club's fairest and best award to Brad Collard.

Clearly his form commanded selection and, having waited an inordinately long time for his opportunity, at least by his own standards, Jakovich was determined to never relinquish his position. Being forced to bide his time might actually have worked to his advantage in the longer term, even if he found that difficult to accept at the time.

"Tim Gepp and Ian Miller, who were on the match committee, kept telling me to hang in there and my chance would come. I just had to maintain my form," Jakovich said. "The worst thing I could have done was drop my bundle because then I would have gone back to South Fremantle and I wouldn't have been switched on.

"Looking back, that 10 week period was probably the best learning experience of my career. But, after winning the Clive Lewington Medal, I remember someone, I think it was South's team manager Santo Pasqua, saying 'that's the last time he'll wear the South Fremantle jumper.' And he was right.

"That period tested my ability to maintain my form, knowing that I received setbacks at the selection table every Thursday night. I thought it didn't worry me; I would just go back and play my best for South. There is nothing you can do, except prove them wrong. I was very single-minded on being an AFL footballer. I didn't play State of Origin football for no reason; I didn't captain the WA Teal Cup team for no reason; I wasn't an All-Australian junior for no reason. So why would I get to the final stepping stone and decide that's too difficult for me?"

As a senior coach in the AFL and particularly as a man in control of a football powerhouse, Mick Malthouse was often asked his views on issues outside the game. He revealed himself to be a staunch environmentalist and was a champion of the cause for old growth forests, among others.

He was also not averse to reminding his players of their social and environmental responsibilities and Glen Jakovich attracted his attention on a couple of fronts.

"No one spent more time in the shower than Glen," Malthouse recounted. "I was always aware of environmental issues and constantly reminded him that we lived on the driest continent in the world. I would walk past him while he was showering, look across and shake my head and he would know what I was on about.

"He would also go shooting and I thought that was fair enough as long as he shot the ferals – things like the wild cats, foxes and rabbits. But he would shoot the Australian fauna and I was always reminding him about those sorts of things as well."

Mick Malthouse

Jakovich accepts that, to a degree, he was a victim of his own high achievements in junior football. Not that success had come easily for him, nothing does. He worked hard for his accomplishments and was immensely proud of his record. When questions were raised by Malthouse about bad habits which had been accepted in the young prodigy, Jakovich accepted the challenge with his trademark verve.

"Who was Mick Malthouse? That was my attitude and I was determined to prove him wrong," Jakovich revealed. "I knew he had question marks and doubts about me, but that's natural, all coaches do. I played my football in a way that was not to his liking, but he did mention it probably wasn't my fault.

"All through my junior football I got into bad habits – that came from playing with kids who were nowhere near my intensity level. My mindset was to go flat out for four quarters where other kids were there to just have fun. When I was playing under 10s it was to win at all costs. It was just full-on competition even when I was playing 12s or 13s. These days it's more diplomatic, where they want to enjoy each other's company and sportsmanship. Back then there was no sportsmanship; the parents on the sidelines used to rush onto the ground to break up fights.

"Fortunately, junior football is a different culture these days. The good kids will still get their chance to shine, but it's more a climate of encouraging every player to be involved in games by rotating them through the positions."

1991: dream becomes a nightmare

IT IS DOUBTFUL whether there has been a bigger occasion in WA football history; certainly from a playing perspective. West Coast had earned the right to play Hawthorn in the first qualifying final of 1991 – it was the first time a final had been played outside of Melbourne.

The euphoria around the State over the match was at fever pitch. West Coast had finished the qualifying rounds on top of the ladder, three games ahead of the Hawks, with a whopping percentage of 162.2. Western Australia was in the grip of finals fever... the attention of the game out-stripped the focus on WA's first State of Origin contest with Victoria in 1977, or subsequent matches in the early and mid '80s where sell-out crowds were virtually guaranteed for Tuesday afternoon matches at Subiaco Oval.

This final with Hawthorn was something else. With superstars like Dermott Brereton, Jason Dunstall, John Platten and Chris Langford, the Hawks were the competition powerhouse. West Coast, with a string of brilliant young guns including Dean Kemp, John Worsfold, Chris Mainwaring, Guy McKenna, Peter Matera and Chris Lewis, were the heir apparent. The hype was breath-taking and, in amongst it all, was a remarkable young defender named Glen Jakovich. This seemed to be a game for which he had been preparing for all his life. But the game of his dreams became a nightmare and one from which he never thought he would recover.

"That '91 season was a fantastic year for my development because so many things happened; the challenge was there to play week in, week out," Jakovich reminisced. "When Hawthorn beat us in the first final played outside of Victoria it made it difficult for us. We finished on top of the table, three games ahead of Hawthorn and the build up to the game was huge.

"At that stage, I had played State of Origin and, because of my youth, it seemed like a very long year. Playing finals at the highest level was obviously new to me, but it was very exciting and it was the unknown to me. I remember Mick saying once that if I couldn't play in the big games I wasn't worth a cold pie to him. That's a pretty daunting thing to say to an 18-year-old and you wouldn't get coaches saying that to kids now. Basically, judgment day came then and there in that game against the Hawks. It was now or never. He was saying something to me that you might expect him to say to a 25 or 30-year-old playing finals football for the first time.

"There was so much hype leading into the Hawthorn game and it got to us. There were 40,000 Craig Turley masks; the pressure went back onto us because Hawthorn were a hardened finals team. They had DiPierdomenico, Tuck, Brereton, Platten, Pritchard... they had premiership players and I was playing my first final.

"For a few guys it was their second finals series, but this was my first experience. I went out there, started in the forward line and then went to the back line. I made a horrible mistake which cost us a goal three minutes before half-time. The ground was muddy, a bit wet underfoot and I took a mark on the left half-back flank, close to where we used to run out on the other side of the ground. Instead of sprinting off the back of the mark, which was the golden rule back then, and peel around, I did my own thing.

"As I marked the ball, I saw Andrew Lockyer leave Jason Dunstall back in the square; he had the whole side of the ground free to himself and could run all the way down that scoreboard wing if I could get it to him. I just screwed it around off one foot, it was a very lazy kick and

Everyone has heard the argument – the West Coast Eagles early success was created by the initial squad being a virtual State team.

Perhaps that might have been true if players like Darren Bewick, Nicky Winmar, Mark Bairstow, Earl Spalding, Warren Dean, Michael Christian and Craig Starcevich stayed in Perth, rather than opting to play with Victorian clubs. Just the same, the early squads did boast some wonderful talent but, as Trevor Nisbett explains, that talent needed to be harnessed and directed, nurtured and cultivated to the point where it was capable of winning a premiership.

"A lot of our players were very good footballers," Nisbett said. "There has been a lot of talk about the club having the players to win more premierships, but I think that is rubbish. The coaching and the club assisted the players throughout the early '90s in winning premierships. The players had to do their job and they did it very well, but I think any of our premiership players who suggest that the players did it all, have got it very wrong. They needed to be disciplined, they needed to follow the match plan, they needed to work to coach's instructions and that's what that group did.

"Plenty of teams have failed to win the premiership when they appeared to have the best players. This team was made up of players who were all very talented within their own right, but they had to conform to a certain strategy and that's what they developed. Glen was able to be the lynchpin and was so creative that we were able to utilise his skills to a maximum. When he was at his best, there was no better player."

Trevor Nisbett

I slipped, kicked it on the inside of my foot and it just trickled along the ground straight into Ben Allan's hands. He walked in and kicked the easiest goal.

"I knew I'd made a huge blunder, but I always confronted people front on. If someone had a criticism of me, I looked them in the eye as if to say 'okay I'll take that on board, but I will prove you wrong or I will make it up to you.' I liked to think I could handle it by saying 'okay, I've made a mistake, but you can still count on me.' That was my philosophy but, after making that mistake on the ground, I made another one when we came off for the half-time break."

Jakovich, with the benefit of hindsight, would certainly have taken a different course of action and deviated from his theory of meeting criticism head-on. Malthouse was furious when the two crossed paths at the half-time break.

"As I look back now, I should have been the last bloke off the ground, but I was the first into the rooms," Jakovich recalled. "Malthouse was waiting for me at the door and grabbed me by the scruff of the neck, took me into the coaches' room, closed the door, pinned me up against the whiteboard and chinned me. He punched me on the chin and said 'If you don't want to play my way, you can pack your bags right now and piss off.'

"That's an edited version of what he said, but it was a savage verbal attack. For the rest of the game, I sat on the bench and watched. I thought the way he had said it that my career was over there and then. I was upset; I was crying after the game and thinking that's it, it's all over for me."

Devastated at missing his perceived long-awaited date with destiny, Jakovich couldn't sleep that night and he spent the next day at work as an apprentice motor mechanic wondering what awaited him that night at training. For the first time in his life, he would have probably preferred to stay back at work, tinkering with a motor, rather than dart off to football training. But, as they say in the classics, a day is a long time in football. Jakovich continues the story:

"It was an amazing 24 hours. We lost the game; the aftermath set in and the media in Melbourne had a field day because we messed up an opportunity to win the first final outside of Melbourne. We lost our double chance and had to front up to a sudden death final against Melbourne at Waverley.

"We'd had some real big battles with Melbourne up to that time. There had been the incident with Chris Lewis and Todd Viney as well as the Jim Stynes – Dwayne Lamb confrontation when Lamby had his arm broken as Stynes tried to hack the ball out of the air, missed and kicked Fatty. So we had all those things confronting us. All day on the Monday after the game against Hawthorn, the talk was who was going to play on Stynes, who, a few weeks later, was crowned a Brownlow Medallist and was the most mobile ruckman going around. Dean Irving was our No.1 ruckman, but he couldn't go with Stynes around the ground.

The perception in other parts of the AFL, particularly Melbourne, was that the West Coast Eagles had a tremendous advantage when it started in an expanded competition in 1987 – it was suggested that the club was a virtual State team playing club sides every week. Perhaps that would have been the case had players like Mark Bairstow, Nicky Winmar, Craig Starcevich, Michael Christian, Warren Dean, Earl Spalding, Peter Wilson, Richard Dennis, Wayne Henwood and others been convinced to play in Perth to be part of an expanded competition. Other clubs also had zones and, while they complained bitterly about the pre-draft selections afforded West Coast as compensation for that situation, which saw the Eagles secure Jakovich and Mitchell White in 1990, the Melbourne clubs had other advantages. For instance, Essendon secured the likes of premiership stars Steven Alessio, Ricky Olarenshaw, Mark Mercuri, Joe Misiti and David Calthorpe through their zone, rather than a draft.

> "Contrary to what Victorian people thought about the club's access to priority players, West Coast secured players like Glen at the expense of a draft selection," Malthouse reflected. "Look at what the Victorian clubs were able to do at that time, for example, I think Essendon picked up Joe Misiti, Ricky Olarenshaw and Mark Mercuri outside the draft. Under the arrangement in place, there was great pressure to make sure we got it right when selecting the priority players out of WA."

Because of that pressure, Malthouse and other key decision makers took plenty of time assessing the claims of the best young talent in WA. History shows that time was well spent, particularly in 1990, with White and Jakovich earning life membership as 150-game players. Both played in premierships and Jakovich will retire at the end of this season as an AFL life member and games record-holder at the West Coast Eagles.

But, given that everything in Jakovich's life happened so quickly, earning State Schoolboys, Teal Cup, South Fremantle and WA selection when his peers were still at school, Malthouse was careful not to rush him into AFL competition. It wasn't that he didn't think Jakovich was capable of playing at the highest level, but he deliberately held him back.

> "I made him wait for his opportunity. I made him a bit more hungry for his opportunity. A lot of things had come easily to him to that point and I thought I could make him appreciate it all the more. I saw what had happened to Stevan Jackson (another precocious young South Fremantle talent) and I didn't want to commit the same mistake with Glen. While his form at South Fremantle was exceptional, I made him do his time at WAFL level."

Mick Malthouse

"A few analysts threw my name in the ring and maybe it got Malthouse thinking. As soon as the Hawthorn game was over, he started planning for Melbourne, going through the videos and books, as he did then. I rocked up to training on the Monday and we had full-on man-to-man, circle work and shepherding. It was a tough session and we were in the middle of a drill called initiative handball when Mick called me over.

"Malthouse had that look in his eye, he was just filthy and no-one dared drop the footy in any of the exercises. I turned up to training with the attitude of not sulking, just to get along and do everything right. Sunday night I was a wreck and struggled at work the next day, but thought the sooner I got to training, the better off I would be. A few people had suggested on radio that I might get the chance to play on Stynes. On one hand, I thought what a great opportunity that would be, but on the other, I thought I'd lucky to be carrying the drinks for the other guys.

"Mick used to call individual players over to him during training and offer a quick assessment of your performance. That was how you did your player interview, on the training track. When he called me, I sprinted over like he was a sergeant in the army. He said 'Are you switched on?' I said 'bloody oath.' And he said 'do you want the job?' Bloody oath!' 'You've got it.'

"That's all he said, except he told me to keep it quiet. Here I was 24 hours earlier thinking I would never play again and now I'm going to play on the best ruckman in the competition. I then remembered his words – 'if you can't play in the big games, then you're not worth a cold pie to me.' I ran with Stynes, played pretty well, even giving him a shiner in a spoiling contest. Within a week, my whole mindset had changed."

After that victory over Melbourne, it was back to Waverley for a preliminary final against Geelong. 'Bleak City', as Melbourne was often referred to in the West, turned on a nasty winter's day even by its own standards.

"It was bitterly cold at Waverley, the coldest day I can ever remember playing footy," Jakovich reflected. "Guys on the bench had buckets of hot water to dip their hands in so they could get some feeling in their fingers. It was a tight game and Suma kicked six in the wet, which was a huge effort, and we booked our first ticket into a grand final.

"When I look back, that grand final against Hawthorn was so disappointing. We had kicked five goals to one with a couple of minutes to go in the first quarter and they kicked a couple in about a minute. We dominated the quarter, but were only up by about 12 points.

"We had been the best side all year, but lost momentum late when beaten by Fitzroy in the last game of the season. No-one could believe we lost that game at Optus Oval. We then lost the first final, won the next two, and lost the grand final when Hawthorn just got on a roll. They physically bashed us after that good start. Mentally, we just weren't up to it and

I remember just sitting out in the middle and I realised the importance of winning and the importance of capitalising on opportunities.

"As we sat in the middle of Waverley, I looked at Michael Brennan, who was vice-captain and a player who didn't show a lot of emotion; he just did his job, was hard as nails and very demanding. To see him in the middle of the oval crying like a baby... and then I looked over and Chris Mainwaring was doing the same. I was over-awed by the whole experience. It had been a big year for me – I'd played 16 games in my first season, played four finals, won rookie of the year, and I now look back on it as a successful year for me personally. It really dawned on me then that, throughout my junior football career, I was always winning individual awards, fairest and bests and I still had that mentality when I was 18, but it was all about team success.

"Mick didn't like that part of my game and it hit me as we were sitting in the middle of the oval. Hawthorn were basking in glory with the premiership cup and I realised that was the reason you played footy – to win that cup and share it with everyone. The experience was great, but it was a wasted opportunity. Okay, they were a great side; a hardened side. But, on our day, we were a better team. Unfortunately, we didn't show it in the most important game of our lives.

"We were the first non-Victorian team in the grand final, so we had to do it our own way and learn from that. In hindsight, we should have gone to Melbourne for the grand final parade, but that's part of being trail-blazers; you make mistakes and learn from them, just as other clubs learn from you. I would have loved to have gone a bit earlier to Melbourne; to be paraded through the streets of Melbourne in a shiny new convertible – it would feel like royalty. But the club made the decision not to go because it didn't fit in with our travel arrangements and we all accepted that. It probably wouldn't have changed the result, but it might have got rid of a few nerves."

1992: grounded Eagles take flight

IF THE EAGLES were brought back to earth by a 1991 grand final defeat, the club was literally grounded when the 1992 campaign hit an unexpected speed hump with an embarrassing first round loss to Sydney. So furious was coach Mick Malthouse with the insipid performance, that he stressed the need for improvement and spent so long dressing down his players that they almost missed the flight from Sydney's Kingsford-Smith Airport. That loss and a similarly unexpected defeat against Fitzroy weeks later, when the club again narrowly avoided missing its flight from Hobart, proved pivotal in what was to be a momentous season.

The general expectation of the football world was that, after losing the grand final against Hawthorn, the West Coast Eagles would be serious contenders a year later. But after that dreadful start to the year, the Eagles status as pre-season premiership favourites diminished. And if the Sydney loss did not lessen expectations, then the ensuing weeks certainly did.

"The first game against Sydney was virtually the top side from the previous year playing the bottom team on the ladder," says Jakovich. "We lost. It was Gary Buckenara's first game as Sydney's coach and we nearly missed the plane after a dressing down from Mick. He was upset and really let the players know it – a few blokes were dropped and others put on notice. That was a wake-up call. Media critics suggested that, because we had lost one grand final, we would win the next. And that was the issue Mick addressed with us.

"Jason Ball had played his first game against the Swans; Trent Nichols made his first appearance after coming from Richmond and, along with Mitchell White and Dean Irving, they were all dropped. Brett Heady and Troy Ugle pinged hamstrings, so there were six changes for the Round 2 clash with St Kilda.

"It was a reality check because everyone expected a flying start and to lose the first game was somewhat disappointing. But it didn't get much better. We had a tough month going to Carrara to play Brisbane in a drawn game and then Richmond at the MCG, where we won by a point, and then down to Hobart to play Fitzroy and got absolutely belted. We also played St Kilda and Geelong at Subiaco Oval, losing to the Cats in Gary Ablett's 150th game. After round six, I think we were eighth on the ladder in a top six system. We had two wins and a draw from six rounds. After Fitzroy, we nearly missed the plane again. We shared the plane with Fitzroy to Hobart and back, seated at the rear of the plane with a livid Malthouse.

"At a meeting after the game, some home truths were pointed out behind closed doors and more players were put on notice. Mick said we were starting to waste our season and, after Fitzroy, four more players were dropped. Trent Nichols was dropped again and so were Daniel Metropolis, Paul Peos and Ryan Turnbull. But it was a game that shaped our season."

Perhaps the players were believing the pre-season publicity and simply assuming the correctness of the popular theory that a team needed to lose a grand final before it could win one. Whatever the problem, it was addressed forcibly at North Hobart Oval and provided the sting which brought a run of success and set up the club's season.

"After losing in Hobart, we won eight of our next nine," Jakovich recounted. "The only loss was against Collingwood at Subiaco Oval on a day when Damien Monkhorst dominated and Craig Kelly did his knee. We were on a roll and our domination at home pretty much returned after that.

"There was another game which could have been a hiccup when we played Footscray at the Western Oval in Round 21. It was a shocking day; they turned the sprinklers on the night before, and it was just one big slosh. We had been playing at Subiaco Oval, the MCG and Waverley on nice, lush surfaces and then we were confronted by this big mud heap. It was rainy and cold and we didn't kick our first goal until time-on in the third quarter.

"It was always going to be hard for us and the conditions suited them beautifully. I suppose it was good to get a bad game out of the way before the finals. We then came home and played Carlton and won well, so we took some confidence into the finals. We thought it would be good to get through the finals and not come up against Hawthorn."

As fate would have it, West Coast couldn't avoid the Hawks and faced their 1991 conquerors at Subiaco Oval again to kick off the finals campaign 12 months after their history-making battle.

"The way it panned out, we got another home final and were pitted against the Hawks again," Jakovich continued. "It was probably one of the biggest games I'd played in because of its importance in the club's history. For the winner, it was the opportunity to advance to a second semi-final; a double chance and a week's rest. For the loser, it was the risk of it being curtains.

"It was a great opportunity to take on the team that had beaten us 12 months earlier. There was so much hype and media about Hawthorn being our bogey side. Yeah, they had beaten us twice in finals in 1991 but, if we were ever going to pin our hat on something, it was that we had learnt from our mistakes and our losses.

"Here we were facing the arch enemy first up in the finals series. We won a classic match by 13 points after the lead had changed something like 14 times during the game. It was such an intense match. I played on Paul Dear, who had won the Norm Smith Medal in the '91 grand final and he played okay, but I had a reasonable day. It was good to beat them at Subiaco Oval; it was more of a relief as well as the satisfaction of proving to ourselves that we could beat them.

"That was a major turning point because we beat the reigning premier, a team which had shown us the way... I suppose the roles were reversed after that game. From there we went into a second semi-final against Geelong and took some momentum forward. We won that by 38 points in front of about 70-odd thousand people at the MCG. Suma kicked eight, Muddy (Waterman) kicked five from half-forward and was fantastic because we went straight into the grand final.

"We had a week's break and, for the second year in succession, we were in the grand final. It was very exciting again. We had two weeks to think about it and talk about it and we went through all the issues of what we had to do to win. There was no compromise and no way we were going to stand in the middle of the ground two years in a row and watch the opposition accept the premiership cup. We didn't want to watch another club hold what was rightfully ours."

Learning from the mistakes

LOSING the 1991 grand final was devastating for the West Coast Eagles. But it would have been even more gut-wrenching had they not learned from the mistakes that contributed to defeat in the club's initial grand final. With people like Mick Malthouse and Trevor Nisbett plotting the club's course, they were always going to remedy the errors of 1991. And, 12 months later, they did.

"We learned from mistakes we made the year before," Jakovich said. "In 1992 we took part in the grand final parade and I'm glad we did; it was a good chance to relax. I remember seeing so many West Australians who had made the journey in the streets of Melbourne. The crowd was dominated by Geelong supporters and Victorian people, but I saw so many West Australians. I recognised people I was acquainted with from back home; sponsors, friends, people I'd seen at training, football-related people. Somehow, so many people managed to get over there. It really hit home that these people had made the effort to get there and see us play and we couldn't let them down. We had an obligation to perform for them; there was no other acceptable result than to win.

"After the parade we went back to the hotel and watched a movie together, relaxed, had a good day and then trained at the MCG. There were puddles of water everywhere and we couldn't believe how good it turned out the next day; one extreme to the other. On grand final day it was so sunny and the ground had drained very well, so it was pretty dry.

"Going in the parade and training on the MCG was a reminder of how special the occasion was. It made you really appreciate the opportunity we had; it was sheer excitement. Once back at the hotel, we got into the normal routine of the team meeting, team dinner, getting a rub and things like that.

"The club booked the 18th floor at the Hilton on the Park and you could see the MCG from your room. At night they had lights on around the ground and I remember looking out a couple of times and thinking that the next day the ground would be packed with about 100,000 people.

"It was only a couple hundred metres from the hotel to the ground and the next day would be the biggest occasion on the football calendar. I remember getting up and watching TV and thinking it has just got to happen. I slept well that night, but grand final day was quite amazing. We used to get up for a jog in the morning to get our bodies moving. It was funny because we used to go about 9am, but by that stage there were already people walking to the ground; getting there early to watch the under 18s and secure their seat for the day.

"We went for a stroll in the park, threw the footy around and had a bit of a kick. But it had already started – there were a lot of Geelong people in jumpers, hats and scarves; they were yelling out a few insults, so it wasn't the normal pre-match routine. There was just a buzz around the place and the pressure was enormous.

"We went back for breakfast and then watched video highlights of ourselves playing good footy and then Trevor Nisbett read out a letter written by Adrian Barich and Phil Scott, players who had been with the club since it started and who had missed out on playing this big game. It was an emotional letter, just saying what it meant to them to see the club in the position of playing in another grand final. While they wished they could be there with us, they wished us well and said all the players who had missed selection were right behind us."

Pint-sized provocateurs

THE NORMAL match-day practice was to have the travelling party of players and officials board a team bus for the trek to the ground. But, on grand final day 1992, it was different. Given that traffic around the ground would be grid-locked, the club decided to walk the group across the park from the hotel to the MCG. It proved an unusual experience and inadvertently provided an extra spur for some of the players.

"When I look back now, it was probably a crazy decision," Jakovich reflected. "We walked over there about midday, with 40,000 people at the MCG; thousands of fans in the car park, with the tray back open on utes and four-wheel drives, having a barbecue and a few VBs.

"You could just imagine how many Geelong supporters had made their way up the highway. They hadn't seen a premiership for almost 30 years and a lot probably weren't even born when the Cats won in 1963. Then they saw the enemy making their way to the arena and, when I look back now, I reflect on how easy it would have been for someone with a few too many under their belt to wander across and kick Peter Matera in the calf or whack Peter Sumich on the leg. It was quite dangerous.

"There were a few taunts directed at us and people were yelling out 'West Coast wankers'. When we lost the 1991 grand final, they must have made up some stickers calling us that and two little kids came up dressed in Geelong jumpers and coats, with their faces painted; their hair painted and they carried Geelong flags. They had that West Coast message plastered on their backs and were running around the players waving the flags under our noses.

"After we ran onto the ground and were 30 seconds away from bounce down in our final huddle, Mainy (Chris Mainwaring) grabbed the blokes and I recall his words: 'Do you remember those two little shits who ran out in front of us? That's what they printed when we lost the grand final last year. There's no way they're going to print that today; it's our time now to fulfil our destiny.' It was pretty stirring stuff coming on top of the pre-game preparations.

"The pre-game warm-up in the rooms was pretty intense; the pressure was immense, but it was no different to the normal routine," Jakovich said. "The game itself was an arm wrestle and they threw everything at us. Pykey was knocked out by Ablett early on and there were a few other scuffles. They came out pretty hard and, to be only two goals up at half-time, we just came in at the break... there was a sense of déjà vu.

"It was like the clock had been wound back 12 months, because when were in a similar position against Hawthorn and Mick was pleading with us, there was just no response. It was a bit too hard. This time Mick didn't have to say anything. We were right in the game and just wanted to get back out there and get the job done. We often talk about that half-time break being pivotal.

"There were certain parts of the year that you look back at, such as when we lost to Fitzroy in Hobart, when we lost by a point against Collingwood and then picked ourselves up off the canvas, when we went down to the Whitten Oval and bounced back from the tactics used there... Then there was the first final and, while everyone else was saying we don't want to play Hawthorn, the players embraced the challenge and wanted to play them. Going to the parade when we hadn't gone the year before was also important. There were so many little incidents or occurrences throughout the season which came back to us at half-time.

"At that stage, we knew there was only an hour left in the season and one team was going to make it and one wasn't. The first 20 minutes of the third quarter were so pivotal. I just remember the steely look in everyone's eyes and there was no way we were going to lose. It was like a group of blokes on death row and we had to fight just to survive. Not a lot was said. All 20 players were calling on themselves to produce something in the second half to avoid being a passenger and we all went to our inner selves to prepare for the second half.

"It was quiet, but very tense. They had thrown everything at us and had so many shots on goal and missed their opportunity. We hadn't fired a shot. Tony Evans kicked a couple of goals just before half-time which dragged the margin back from four goals down to two and it was fantastic.

"There was a phenomenal feeling at the start of the third quarter, the premiership quarter. We played our best footy. Roo (Matera) was sensational, Evo (Evans) kicked another magnificent goal, Boris (Langdon) did a couple of courageous things, Willo produced the cork in the ocean goal, Suma steadied and was calm in the crisis. The half-back line was rock solid. We shut them down, Milli continued to stay on top of Brownless, Pykey courageously came back on. There was just no way he was going to surrender.

"That was just a very powerful moment. We felt we could achieve anything when we put our minds together. It was so unique to be involved in that and the result looked after itself. Mick never worried about the result specifically. For him, it was about the method. That second half could have gone on for three weeks, but we just had control of what we were doing. We only won by four goals, but that was not a true reflection."

So decisive was the team performance in the third quarter that most people outside of those directly involved at Geelong probably considered the game over but, for the Eagles, it was a matter of continuing the process.

"People thought we had it won at three-quarter time, but because Mick had us so focused I wasn't convinced until I saw my lunatic captain running around with four or five minutes to go," Jakovich reminisced.

"We were trading possessions; no-one was scoring goals and fatigue was starting to kick in. We'd been playing 115 minutes of a 120 minute game and they were gone. I was just so focused; I was playing on a key player in Barry Stoneham and I just thought 'every time it comes down here I have to man up; I have to spoil; run; create.' Then Woosha was running around with this chirpy little voice; running past all the boys and he was just so pumped and excited. You had to be there to experience it, but he was not talking about manning up like he normally would. That's why he broke my focus. He had this big smile on his face and was saying 'we've got 'em, we've got 'em.'"

"There was this big out-pouring of emotion. He was just high on emotion and I looked at him and realised we were going to win the grand final. The next five minutes were the best five minutes of my life because the game was still in play, but I knew we had won it. Then I went through all the little moments in the season and thought about being crowned as the champions. I was thinking I'm going to get a medal; we're going to get a cup. Meanwhile the game was still going on.

"I tried to run forward to see if I could kick a goal. You do some silly things. When that siren went, Suma was running towards me and carrying on. I thought what's going on with these blokes. Woosha was carrying on like a lunatic and Suma was just screaming my name out. Me, Suma and Boris (Langdon) were the first to embrace and, before I knew it, there was just one big pile of blokes climbing all over each other. The staff joined in and the coach was down by then and it was just an overflow of emotion. It was all such a high because it was the first time. All of us getting our medals, Roo winning the Norm Smith was so fitting, then the presentation of the cup and I can just remember seeing relief on their faces.

"I can remember the lap of honour with everyone trying to identify people in the crowd. I saw a few friends that I ran over to... doing the lap honour to the tune of *We are the Champions* was just phenomenal.

"Back in the rooms, it was chaotic. All the wives and girlfriends came down and my brother came in, even though he was a Melbourne player; he'd gone to the grand final and it was quite interesting. He said he didn't want to go down, but just had to. He said he was glad he did, but he didn't stay long; he felt that he just had to see his brother and offer me congratulations. That was special. Obviously, he had his alignment with his teammates and his club. The fact that our Dad had died three years earlier was also very emotional for me. If he had been there to see his son on the biggest stage of all, it would have been so special.

"There were so many people and players off in side rooms trying to escape all the commotion in the main changerooms. Suma peeled off with the cup and sat down with trainers Billy Sutherland and Dave Jones. There's a photo of Suma with them, holding up the cup and he just wanted a moment with it.

"Suma's not normally an emotional bloke, but when I looked at him, he was just spent. He sat down and just stared at the cup. I could appreciate where he was coming from, but for me it was the other way. I was on so much of a high, but looking back now I can understand the pressure on him. He was a much-maligned full-forward who missed a couple of shots early, but kicked six in the biggest game of our lives. He had a terrific finals series and that was awesome for him. Then, someone like Tony Evans, stepped up to centre stage after being in and out for much of the year and there was some doubt as to whether he would make it. Not only that, but he would become a household name."

After basking in the glory with teammates, friends, relatives and club officials, it was time to take the celebration to the people – the thousands of West Australians who had journeyed east to witness history. The club had booked the Glasshouse, a big venue just a short walk from the MCG, for the post-match activities and the players were greeted by thousands of jubilant fans, a virtual sea of blue and gold as they were introduced one by one.

"The Glasshouse was just unbelievable," Jakovich said. "They left us on stage because there was no way we could go into the crowd; if we'd gone there we would be still there. I suppose, from the point of view of the fans, that might have been disappointing, but it was just pandemonium. We then went back to the Hilton and had the official grand final dinner. That really was special. Terry O'Connor, who was our chairman, made an amazing speech about history being created. It was just a buzz. The band got cranked up and everyone was into it. There were some funny stories after it.

"The best thing I did was enjoy it a little bit, but then I went to bed and made sure I got at least four or five hours' sleep. I had an inkling of what would be waiting for us back in Perth the next day and I thanked my lucky stars I did because, when we got to the airport, there were some guys who hadn't been to bed. They looked pretty average. The club booked a seat in first class for the cup, which I thought was pretty funny. A few guys had a beer or two on the way home, but there were a lot of guys sleeping too. When we arrived in Perth, it was everything I had expected... and more. Having a police escort after a bus came out on to the tarmac to pick us up, I felt like the president of the United States or the Beatles.

The Jakovich boys were like any other family unit. Be it backyard football, cricket or tiddly winks, it was highly competitive. Rules were cast to off-set the age difference and sledging was cultivated courtesy of the family battle. Long before Glen and Allan competed against each other in the public domain of the AFL, they had endured many intense contests in the privacy of their own home. Those domestic affairs, just like many thousands of others across the country, were the genesis of modified rules in various sports, although those who govern the game might not have sanctioned the exchange of barbs between the Jakovich boys.

In the main, they were good humoured jibes, aimed at getting a point across, but camouflaged by a splash of wit. And that family rivalry was there for all to see at the MCG in a qualifying round match in 1991. The two Jakovich boys had previously played against each other in a State game, when Allan represented South Australia in 1990, but the next time they crossed paths on the football field it created a headline or two.

After Allan had kicked a goal for Melbourne late in the game, he gave his younger brother a kiss on the head. It was a move which infuriated Eagles skipper John Worsfold, who left no doubt as to his feelings as he confronted the senior Jakovich. But Allan thought it was just a bit of fun; an extension of the backyard antics.

"The next time I played against Glen was when I was playing for Melbourne in 1991," he said. "The first time we played that season was at Subiaco Oval in Round 1 and the team only kicked two goals. But the return game was at the MCG. That was the day I

We went straight to Subiaco Oval and I can remember seeing people lining the streets from the airport. It was just remarkable.

"People were tooting their horns, Eagles balloons and scarves in their hands, just waiting for us to drive past. When we got to Hay Street, it was just packed and when we got to Subiaco Oval I had never seen so many people in my life."

It was at the Subiaco Oval assembly where Jakovich made his own mark on the celebrations.

"I sang a little ditty," he said. "When I played junior footy, we sometimes got belted and won one game in about three years. It was all driven by the Mums and Dads, who peeled the oranges, washed the jumpers. One of the players' Dad was a helper around the team and we won a game, our first in three years, and he sang that song. I remembered learning it

kissed Glen on the head. Mum was there for that game too. I had just kicked a point and followed up pretty quickly with my seventh goal and we were behind by a point as I was lining up at the city end of the ground with Glen standing on the mark. We used to call each other 'young man' for some reason and Glen stood the mark and was calling that out trying to put me off. When we were kids we had also watched *The Exorcist* and that had really frightened Glen. We were Catholic and the movie freaked him out a bit, but he remembered a few choice lines from the movie and was throwing them at me.

"I missed as the ball faded after it looked pretty good off the boot. John Worsfold kicked the ball in to Guy McKenna, who tried to chip it over my head, but I managed to intercept it. Glen stood on the mark again and was yelling out some pretty obscene stuff from *The Exorcist*. I remember Jimmy Stynes walking behind Glen and he was just shaking his head, he couldn't believe what was being said. I kicked the goal and I suppose it was a rush of blood, but I then gave Glen a bit of a smooch on the head.

"After the game we were in my car going back to my place. Mum was sitting in the front and Glen was in the back and we just had a bit of a chuckle about that incident, but I thought mum was struggling with it a bit. Again, it hadn't been that long since Dad had passed away and I could feel the old girl was struggling. I didn't know what to say and I looked across at the old girl and she was crying. I looked in the rear vision mirror and Glen was crying as well and I joined them pretty soon after that. Dad wasn't mentioned once on the trip to Williamstown all the way over the Westgate Bridge, but he was certainly in all of our thoughts."

Allan Jakovich

and thought that, if we won the grand final, I would sing that song. I sang it everywhere; on the team bus after the game and then Mick asked me to sing it again. All of a sudden, I had to sing it everywhere I went.

"I finished third in the club champion award that year and, in my first two years, I had played in two grand finals for a premiership. That was when I felt I had made it as a player. Mick started to believe in me and I started to repay that faith. I sat back after that season and thought I'd played only 40 games and been in two grand finals. I was only 19 years of age. How good was that!"

While Jakovich carved out a wonderful career, his mother was always there supporting him. Sometimes, when Allan was playing with Melbourne and Glen was with West Coast, it was difficult. She supported neither team, just her boys.

"In 1992 it was just unbelievable," she reflected. "Even before Glen came out, just the atmosphere was electric and something I had never experienced. I had never been to a grand final before and, in 1994, I was up high in the stands. While it was great, it wasn't as good as the first one.

"I was back at the dinner at the Hilton after the 1992 premiership when Glen spoke to me the first time and he was very proud and happy. When they lost in 1991, I couldn't live with him, he was moping around. I said 'Glen what's wrong?' and he said 'I've got to live with this for the rest of my life.' I told him if that was the biggest problem in his life, he didn't have anything to worry about. But football is his life. I know it has to come to an end, but I don't know how he will cope.

"When Allan and Glen played against each other, I was always at the ground. The Demons meant as much to me as the Eagles at that stage and I couldn't go for the Demons more than the Eagles, although Allan probably wouldn't believe me. If the Eagles were kicking for goal, I would hope they would kick it. And if the Demons were kicking for goal, I would hope they would kick it. The day that Allan kissed Glen, I was very proud and I was there when a Melbourne supporter said 'make up your mind woman.' Then he must have figured it out. I must have called out 'Go Allan or go Glen' and he worked it out that I was barracking for my boys. They say you can't win, but you can't lose either."

Mary Jakovich

1993: a year wasted

AS PEOPLE reflect on the achievements of the West Coast Eagles in the early and mid-1990s, the team has often been accused of under-performing. With the talent in the group, it has been suggested that the club should have won at least one more premiership. Glen Jakovich, the cornerstone of a wonderful defence in that era, agrees. But he also concedes there were mitigating circumstances. Jakovich reckons that inexperience within the club and the player group after the 1992 triumph contributed to a missed opportunity in 1993.

"After winning in '92 it was unchartered waters for us as the reigning premiers," Jakovich suggested. "Our pre-season wasn't as intense as it had been the previous year, which had an effect on the player group. We weren't fit enough come finals time and other sides seemed to have an edge on us. We lost a few games and just battled to get into the final six, as it was then. We made it on percentage.

"It was a year wasted. Basically, we still had the same player group together. We played North in the first final, which we won, but then had to play Essendon in Melbourne, even though the Bombers lost in the first week, and they bundled us out. That draw really hurt us and helped Essendon to the point where they probably won a premiership ahead of their time with a group dubbed the 'baby bombers.'

"I felt we were better than Essendon, but I suppose Kevin Sheedy won a psychological battle as well when he called on all Victorian footy fans to get behind them when they played us. He did it well. They had enormous support at the MCG and, while we were accustomed to playing in front of hostile crowds, that was very much a lop-sided crowd.

"When we sat down after that game, Mick hammered it home as to what he thought about it all and that a few players weren't hungry enough. A few of the guys were enjoying the lifestyle; they had been signed on longer-term contracts and Mick thought outside influences had taken over a little. Actually, he was quite adamant about not allowing those things to take control. It was a poor year on and off field because there weren't a lot of functions organised for the players either."

1994: a catalyst for success

Pre-season Gold Coast party

IMAGINE a group of AFL players heading off to the Gold Coast in the first week of December for a swim through which had nothing to do with enjoying the surf. It was a journey of fun and frivolity. It just wouldn't happen today but, only a decade ago, such a trip proved pivotal in the journey of the West Coast Eagles to the 1994 premiership.

It was late November 1993 when a posse of senior players, including John Worsfold, Dwayne Lamb and Michael Brennan, met with coach Mick Malthouse and senior management to discuss their plan. The players felt it was needed to break up the monotony of pre-season training and to help bring the playing group together.

"There was no players' trip organised, as there had been in the previous two years," Jakovich said. "The senior group, led by John, Michael and Dwayne, was still very strong, and felt it was pivotal for us to get away to a solid start in 1994.

"So we felt we needed a holiday. It was in the middle of December and we asked for a holiday and Mick was just livid, but he bowed to the senior group and allowed it to happen. That player trip was one of the best trips I've ever been on because it underlined everyone's commitment to the club. As you do every night on a players' trip, you are out until all hours yahooing and having a great time. But at 10am every day we had to meet at the beach. The hotel was about 5-6km from the central part of the Gold Coast strip, but there was seldom anyone in any condition to run.

"We had to push ourselves through the pain barrier because we felt that, even though we were on a footy trip, we had to keep some sort of fitness up; we couldn't just go up there and relax. Every night we were burning the midnight oil... we called it the 'what's going on tour.' We had tee-shirts and stubby holders made and there was a lot of effort put into it by the player group. The players got off their backsides and brought the younger guys together.

"We did little things like have a younger guy and a senior player share a room, just helping the new blokes to become familiar and comfortable within the group. Every night we went out together as a group, whereas these days on footy trips guys go off in every direction, but we stuck together. I felt we won the 1994 flag because of that underlying commitment.

"Every morning we would run 6-8km, do sit-ups and push-ups and punish ourselves in quite draining conditions. Then we would get out on the town again at night, but I think it proved pivotal because we had wasted 1993. Speaking to a lot of players from 1994, the success stemmed back to December 2 when we made the commitment to each other on the trip."

Footy trips create some lasting memories and the Gold Coast excursion was no exception.

"We had only been at our hotel for about 10 minutes when I saw Tony Evans wander across the road to a service station," Jakovich reflected. He came back with a big hose and a funnel and I wondered what they were for. I knew he didn't have a vehicle, so he wouldn't have any fuel problems. I soon found out what it was all about and it played a key role in the rest of the trip as we engaged in a few drinking games.

"Evo (or Barney) even bought a 'G' clamp because there was obviously the risk of losing too much fluid from the join between the hose and the funnel as the boys aimed to help the fluid flow down the hatch. Barney was a master of doing things like that and they went a long way towards building the team bond. That trip was the foundation on which the success of 1994 was built."

The season continues

THE SEASON went pretty well for West Coast, right from the start. The Eagles finished on top of the ladder and won the McLelland Trophy as the minor premiers, earning two home finals. It was also the season of that infamous brawl at Subiaco Oval against Footscray in the last qualifying game of the season.

"That was quite interesting because we had five guys cited and the opposition started the fight, which made it hard for us to understand," Jakovich said. "It was the week before our first final, which had an emotional bearing on us leading into the Collingwood game, which we only won by a few points. We didn't know who was available until late in that week because proceedings dragged right through until Friday and we needed to prepare ourselves for a Sunday game. To have those things pending so deep into the week was distracting. Footscray took out a Supreme Court injunction, but we went ahead and faced the tribunal. We wanted it out of the way. The West Coast players cited were myself, Suma, Don Pyke, Chris Lewis and Jason Ball.

"It happened as the match was getting spiteful and Steve Wallis knocked out Brett Heady. There was a bit of remonstration and then it was on. Before you knew it, there was a big mêlée and Suma had the big sleeper hold put on him by Daniel Southern... he lost consciousness and was stretchered off.

"The air of invincibility around that player group was enormous because we came in at half-time and Suma was still out on the ground getting medical attention. We were all sitting down when he came through the race on a stretcher with an oxygen mask on his face, which generated more emotion. We had seen one of our own in a bad way and we considered it so serious he might even have been fighting for his life. When you see one of your mates wearing an oxygen mask, surrounded by paramedics and doctors, you start to wonder what's going on. Suma blacked out from a lack of oxygen to the brain and it was quite serious.

"When Mick came through to talk to the players, he was very emotional, saying they'd had a crack at one of ours from behind and had started it. Then we went out and belted them both physically and on the scoreboard. Footscray were quite surprised at how physically imposing we were after the break, but that was a hallmark of our team. If ever we were challenged in that sense, we stood up and gave it back with interest. If anyone tested us in that vein, we would step up our level of play and show them we wouldn't be challenged. It was very satisfying to be a part of that, but the tribunal was a big distraction."

Towards the finals

WITH a dozen players charged after the mêlée, it was big news leading into the finals and something neither club enjoyed. Footscray sought and received a stay of proceedings, but West Coast wanted to deal with it as soon as possible; however, it still wasn't resolved until late in the week and removed some of the focus for the five players on report – it was anything but ideal.

"The final against Collingwood at the WACA ground will probably be best remembered for an incident after the siren involving Micky McGuane and John Worsfold," Jakovich explained. "Woosha said something to Micky, tongue in cheek, which wasn't too well received. We had been in a bit of trouble during the game and they had a strong breeze at their backs in the last quarter and came home pretty hard.

"McGuane was a great player, but enjoyed a sledge; he could talk the talk and, as they came at us in the dying stages, he delivered a verbal jibe at our skipper. I thought he was pretty game taking that attitude to Woosha. Our season was in serious danger because, if we lost to Collingwood, we would have to travel to Melbourne and it would cost us the week's break. To win the flag from there, we would have had to travel to Melbourne three weeks in a row.

"McGuane kept running up to Woosha, Bluey McKenna and myself yelling 'you blokes are gone, you blokes are gone.' He was basically calling us chokers, saying you blokes are freezing. At the time the pressure was so intense, but John didn't take the bait and I suppose that is why we won. We had to stay focused. We didn't have the luxury of being five goals up and having this bloke in our ear. He was getting in our ear because he believed they were going to cause the biggest upset of the year. As it turned out, they fell two points shy and Woosha, who had withstood the verbal barrage, saying nothing, saying nothing, saying nothing. Until the final siren. But when that siren sounded, he went to Micky McGuane and said 'two points short, have a good pre-season.'

"Micky didn't like it. Emotions were running high because they had missed a magnificent opportunity and, given another minute or two, we probably would have lost. The siren couldn't come quickly enough. Also, near the end of the game, Micky dropped a chest mark so maybe his focus wasn't on the footy and maybe that's why he dropped it. He was also staring straight into the sun, so it wouldn't have been easy to see. When he dropped the mark, Don Pyke and myself pounced on it and locked it up. There were only a few seconds left on the clock. After that we were home."

The premiership assault

AFTER two eventful weeks playing at home, one at Subiaco and the other at the WACA ground, the launching pad had been set for the premiership assault. The second home final against Melbourne was also scheduled for cricket headquarters because Subiaco Oval was undergoing extensive re-development work.

"We were convincing winners against Melbourne," Jakovich reflected. "And then we were in the grand final against Geelong. In that grand final we were always in control. By the end of 1994 I had played in two premierships and three grand finals and won a best and fairest in a premiership season, which was probably my greatest individual achievement. I was also selected in the All-Australian team for the first time and I was only 21. It was quite fantastic to have achieved all that in such a short space of time.

"The grand final was in stark contrast to 1992, although Geelong came out hard at us, which we expected. At quarter-time, we were up by a point and they got back into the game with two or three quick goals. But even at quarter-time we knew we had them covered. We came in at half-time and were four or five goals up... it should have been more like eight goals. We ended up kicking 20.23 for the game, so there were 43 scoring shots and we wasted a few opportunities. It would have been a disappointing grand final from a spectator's point of view. I have since watched the replay and it's not a very good game. Even our play was a bit frustrating because we weren't kicking goals until the last quarter, when we had an eight-goal term and won by 80 points.

"The feeling among the players on that day was one of invincibility and, I suppose, arrogance. I remember at three-quarter time having a joke with Suma. As much as we were supposed to be focused, I think we were up by seven goals, we had a joke at the back of the huddle. We just felt we were in full control. We were red-hot favourites and it felt like a foregone conclusion. It was great for David Hart and David Hynes because they had missed out in 1992. Dhuf did a hamstring playing for South Fremantle, so I was really happy for him and Hynesy was also a popular player. I was also pleased for a few of the new guys who had come into the team like Drew Banfield, Ryan Turnbull and Shane Bond. It was great to have other players enjoy premiership success.

"We had a good mix of players. Peter Wilson was fantastic right through the year and played very well in the grand final, kicking a couple of important goals in the second quarter. One of my great memories of the grand final was Michael Brennan keeping Gary Ablett to only a couple of touches. It would be fair to say that Monkey had a disappointing 1992 grand final and he had set himself for a big game in 1994. Jason Ball played in his first grand final as well and put in a great game.

"That year I was one of the favourites for the Brownlow Medal and it was good to be recognised for my year. But, when the votes were counted, Greg Williams won quite easily from Peter Matera. In any other year, with the number of votes Roo polled (29), he would have won the Medal. I only polled 12 votes, which was a little bit disappointing, but I had greater things to focus on that week and that was to win another premiership. I remember sitting down on the Sunday and Monday after the grand final, glancing down at my premiership medal and thinking that this is the real reason you play the game."

1995: a let down year

AFTER being the competition benchmark in the initial years of the 1990s, the West Coast Eagles again failed to live up to expectations immediately after winning the 1994 grand final. There was a subtle changing of the guard with the retirement of a number of senior players, including premiership heroes Michael Brennan, Peter Wilson and Paul Harding, but the air of invincibility lifted as well.

Glen Jakovich saw that as a broad shift. The departure of those stars, combined with the emergence of other clubs to challenge the Eagles, saw teams like North Melbourne and Carlton take up the running.

"Two teams passed us in 1995 as we had a let-down year and a few guys moved on to create a turn-over of players," Jakovich said. "We lost a large slice of experience and most other teams were coming at us because we were the benchmark. Not only did they reach us, but a couple of teams went past us. Carlton had a great year and the Kangaroos emerged on the way to dominating the second half of the '90s. From a personal point of view, I played every game, won my third best and fairest and was selected in the All-Australian team again.

"I approached the year the same as I did in '92 and '93. I wanted to have a mammoth pre-season, which I did, and then went out and tried to beat my opponent every week so I could contribute to the team. We were very inconsistent that year, I suppose we were never quite there mentally and we made a straight sets exit out of the finals.

"It is hard to back up a premiership, but I thought the player group in '95 was still quite awesome; we certainly should have done better. We only lost to Carlton at Subi by a point in a classic game late in the season, which I felt we should have won. It came at a crucial time, just two games out from the finals, and I felt we needed to beat them from a psychological point of view. They were a great side and only lost two games for the year and deservedly won the grand final."

Demolition Derby

While the 1995 season saw West Coast finish fifth, the year was significant from another perspective with the arrival of an inter-town competitor, the Fremantle Dockers. It was a different experience for the Eagles players, where the spotlight, which had been solely focused on them, was suddenly shared. Some enjoyed that shift in focus, but there was still a strong desire to ensure that West Coast remained the dominant force. And, if there was any doubt about how the West Coast players were thinking, it came in the first Western Derby.

"The first Derby was quite a big occasion because we had the opening of the new grandstand at Subiaco Oval and we were confronted with the new team on the block, our new arch rival," Jakovich said. "The Prime Minister, Paul Keating, officially opened the stand and he was in the rooms before the game shaking hands with the players, which was quite an honour. So those types of things were quite interesting.

"Fremantle were going all right when we played them. I remember there was an enormous amount of media hype surrounding the game and there was a big photo taken of all the players lining up on the ground before the bounce. It was a whitewash in the end, though. I think we won by 80 odd points and asserted our authority from the outset. That performance was player driven rather than an instruction from the coach.

"I started on Peter Mann and also played on Craig Burrows but, every time the Dockers players went near the ball, we exerted some physical pressure on them by tackling and trying to drive them into the ground. We wanted to show them the intensity required in AFL football. We had lost the week before against Carlton and we really wanted to get some form. It just happened to be against Fremantle. Woosha got hold of Winston Abraham and I've never seen a young bloke so intimidated. Woosha always gave the impression he wanted to kill his opponent, but he was really just a fierce competitor. He felt he had to exert his physical presence every time the ball approached; we needed to protect our turf. John was part of our initial team, along with blokes like Chris Lewis and Michael Brennan, and they copped a few hidings in their initial years as well.

"We kicked 1.12 against Essendon in 1989 and had some rough games at Princes Park and they learned some tough lessons. John was never a sniper and he only ever took his eyes off the ball when we had possession and then he would be preparing to lay a block or a shepherd. He did that with great force and talent, but he also knew how to get the footy and was a very important player for us.

"The second Derby was the last qualifying game of the season and we won by about nine goals and went on to play Essendon in the first final. We lost to them – that was very disappointing because we had our chances to win and I just don't think we were hungry enough. Because we lost, we had to go back to Melbourne and play North and we lost that as well. We were a good enough side to do better than that, and it was the first time we'd bowed out of a finals series in straight sets. North actually gave us a belting and we were never in that game. It was a very empty way to finish a season."

Fremantle foes

It might sound a little like the clichéd Wild West showdown, but the arrival of a new AFL franchise in Perth really did cramp the style of the West Coast Eagles. It did not stretch to the point of drawn pistols at dawn, but there was a sense that this town was not big enough for two clubs. The WA turf had belonged to the West Coast Eagles before the addition of the Fremantle Dockers in 1995 and the two-time premiers were determined to make sure their new arch-rivals were aware of where they sat in the pecking order.

That much was evident on field when the Eagles flexed their muscles, quite literally, in winning the first nine Western Derbies. But with every victory the club was aware it was nearing its first defeat, because that sort of domination does not last indefinitely. Everyone knew that Fremantle would eventually break through and that happened in the 10th Western Derby on Sunday July 18, 1999.

While that game sticks in the craw of West Coast Eagles players, those within the team when Fremantle was admitted into the competition made a pact that they did not want to be part of the first team to lose to Fremantle. In winning the first nine clashes West Coast made good that pledge, but even that dominance was not completely enjoyed by the players.

> "It was great to win those early games, but you really can't say they were fantastic Derbies," Jakovich said. "I say that because I grew up in a culture of Derbies at South Fremantle and you wouldn't even drive through the streets of East Fremantle in the week of a Derby. You would by-pass East Fremantle and go the long way to training or home. There was 100 years of tradition in those games and playing against East Fremantle it didn't matter where you were on the premiership table, it was rarely a one-sided event. I grew up with that at school and played in six Derbies while at South Fremantle, for a 4-2 record, which I'm quite proud of. I played in a final when we beat them so that was even sweeter.

> "The Western Derbies are fantastic and you can go to Subiaco Oval and sometimes be booed. It's a different feeling, but knowing there is another passionate group of supporters out there makes it more interesting. I'm probably in the middle of it all because I am a true Fremantle person. I'm probably more Fremantle than most of the players who have played for them. I went to school there, I played my junior football there and had my first job there. To me, I hold the Derbies special and we've had some great battles.

"The build-up is a little over the top and we, as players, acknowledge that it's only one game and you don't get any more out of it in terms of four premiership points. You don't hang your hat for an entire season on winning a Derby and I dare say Fremantle feel the same way. I'd be more than happy to lose two Derbies in a season if it meant we went on to win the premiership. Having said that, we put a lot of energy and attention into setting ourselves for a Derby. The guys really look forward to it, but the key is not getting too caught up in the build up of it all, although in this town that's difficult because every corner you turn someone will be there talking about the game.

"From that aspect, it has been shown that the guys sometimes get over the top with the build-up, but it should be measured on the quality of the games. If you look at the last one in Round 22, 2003 the lead changed so many times and it was a great game, but unfortunately Fremantle got up and won. But who could forget Daniel Kerr's run from half-back which eventually won him the goal of the year? Paul Hasleby's interception clinched the game for them and he won the Ross Glendinning Medal. People talk about those matches, both before and after, for a long time and that has to be good for the game."

While the tradition in Derbies has evolved over the last decade, the first contest between the two clubs will always hold fond memories for Jakovich.

"I always reflect on the first Derby as the most memorable," he said. "Having the Prime Minister (Paul Keating) in the rooms before the match shaking hands with the players was a highlight and the opening of the new grandstand was a significant landmark in WA football history. It also meant that for a relatively small population WA was able to field two teams in the AFL competition and that was an achievement. It was a big landmark in WA football, which marked a special place in a 100-plus year history of the game here. The redevelopment of the ground, the emergence of Fremantle and the game itself were significant in the evolution of football in this State.

"There was a game where Scott Cummings kicked 10 goals and we beat them by 119 points. They are never good games to be on the wrong end of and, fortunately, I haven't experienced a hiding like that at the hands of Fremantle, but I have experienced losses of that magnitude and I can tell you it's no fun.

"That game sticks in my mind because we won so convincingly and Cummo was the first player to kick 10 in a Derby. There was a game where Fido (Phil Matera) kicked seven goals and we were about 40 points up at three-quarter time. We just hung on and some would say the better team lost on the day, but we went on to win six games on the trot after that so it set our season up. It was a tough one, but we hung in there and pinched every second goal. Coming off that game was real satisfying.

"There was the game against Fremantle when I was reported for striking Trent Croad. I was suspended, but appealed and had the decision over-turned. I played my best-ever game the week after that, against Collingwood. There was turmoil and controversy, but I was pleased to keep my record clean.

"I was just a little frustrated. We were playing good football, but made some silly mistakes which allowed Fremantle back into the game and they got the ascendancy. Then I did a stupid thing. I just went to push him away and ended up making contact with his face. Before I knew it there was a 50-metre penalty, he kicked a goal and the three-tier stand was going off. I had about six Fremantle players in my face and just wanted to disappear because I knew I had messed up. That happens in Derbies and, unfortunately, I was on the wrong end of it. I was tagged Slapovich by some of the Fremantle fans, which was quite humorous."

Jakovich still remembers vividly the inauguration of the rivalry and he felt his team had an edge, not because the club had just won its second premiership when Fremantle entered the competition, but because he considered the Dockers to be less than professional.

"When the AFL accepted Fremantle into the competition – whether it was the media or the players – our pre-game mindset was to never lose to those blokes down the road," he said. "They were the new boys on the track and I guess we had a fair amount of arrogance in that we had just won two premierships and were the premier team in the competition, let alone worry about who was going to be the dominant team from Perth.

"We had always set very high levels of professionalism and that was why we achieved what we did, while Fremantle took a more low-key approach. Gerard Neesham's style was a much-publicised method of training and we saw footage of them going onto the track in board shorts and tank tops and they didn't even look like a professional AFL outfit. In our pre-game build-ups we used to say 'these guys are nowhere near the mark.' We were always trying to find kinks in the armour of the opposition, not just Fremantle, but any opponent. And that unprofessional appearance was one area Mick highlighted in relation to the Dockers.

"We won the first nine Derbies and there were some big games where we won quite convincingly, while there were others in the late part of the '90s where they got close. But the sheer fact that we didn't want to lose to them kicked in and we found a way to win.

"When they finally did beat us, players like Chris Bond, Adrian Fletcher and a few of the senior guys at Fremantle said 'hang on we've had enough of this, let's give it back to them.' And they beat us in '99 when we kicked the first three goals of the game. Since then it has become the way Derbies should be, it's a bit more even."

1996: the emperor falls

NO-ONE ever imagined that Glen Jakovich would be cut down. By anything. Not by an opponent, not by injury and not by his own failure to give himself every opportunity to succeed. The West Coast Eagles colossus stood at centre half-back like some ancient Roman ruler. You could picture this man in the days of the Roman empire, standing proud in his toga which gave way to massive thighs, gold plates wrapped around his imposing wrists, scabbard draped from his hips. On the east coast, Jakovich's imposing physical presence saw him tagged Robocop. He seemed indestructible; bullet proof.

But, in one devastating second at Subiaco Oval in 1996, that image was destroyed. As he twisted and tried to turn, his right knee gave out beneath his imposing frame. He grabbed at the joint instinctively, rose to his feet and tried to continue. But this was no flesh wound; nothing he could simply brush aside, ignore and resume. The emperor was wounded.

"The 1996 pre-season was good," recalls Jakovich. "I was fit and enjoying the season when, in my 96th consecutive game, I picked up the footy at half-back against St Kilda, twisted and turned and my knee buckled underneath me. It was just a quick twist and I felt this uncomfortable pain in my knee. It wasn't excruciating, just uncomfortable.

"I knew I was in trouble and then I tried to get up to take a boundary throw-in. One of the St Kilda players went at the ball and I just couldn't go with him. I couldn't move and I knew I was in trouble.

"But, when my body temperature came down, I felt good. I said to the docs I felt good enough to go back on. But they said no, just give it a rest. So I put a tracksuit on and sat down and the knee just seized up. I went down the race after the game and the knee buckled again, so obviously the anterior cruciate ligament was shot. It couldn't support my knee on that gentle decline to the rooms.

"The orthopaedic surgeons were at the game and came down and gave my knee what they call a pivot shift test to see how much 'play' there was in the joint. There should only be a certain amount of 'play' – if you have snapped or torn the anterior cruciate ligament, it becomes very loose. The pivot shift test was considerably loose and they told me pretty well straight away that my season was over.

"I was quite devastated. They said I'd need an arthroscopy and, if it wasn't too bad, they would close it up and it would be a six-12 week injury. But if it was what they thought it was – and they were 99.9 percent sure it was – they would do the reconstruction and I'd be out for 12 months."

Although Jakovich realised the severity of the situation, he could not accept it. Football was his life and nothing or no-one would ever take it from him. This time he was powerless. He had played against – and beaten – some of the great luminaries of his time; players like Wayne Carey, who would forever be revered as one of the finest players the game has seen. Jakovich also had difficulty accepting that he would be consigned to a 12-month rehabilitation. He was emotional when television cameras camped outside the change rooms waiting for him to hobble the 15 or 20 metres on crutches to the car park.

"I was a bit annoyed when I left the ground after the match when a couple of TV cameras were in my face," he said. "I felt that I deserved a little more respect. The cameras had these bright lights on them which made it difficult for me to see as well. I had just been told of my fate and I suppose I lashed out at them in frustration. In hindsight, I probably said a few things to them that I shouldn't have. One minute, everything is going along nicely; I'm playing good footy, hadn't missed a game for a while, had played in premierships, enjoyed a lot of individual success and, the next thing, I've done my anterior cruciate ligament through a simple twist on the footy field.

It was Round 12, 1996 against St Kilda at Subiaco Oval when Glen Jakovich twisted and dodged, as he had done millions of times. Only this time his right knee buckled beneath him. The anterior cruciate ligament was ruptured and a man who seemed invincible suddenly became vulnerable, leaving the West Coast match committee with a problem they had not envisaged – replacing Jako.

Trevor Nisbett knew immediately that Jakovich was in trouble and knew also that it would mean finding a replacement within the squad for the remainder of the 1996 campaign as well as the initial stages of the 1997 season.

"I knew he had done his knee. It was pretty obvious," Nisbett recalled. "But the one thing about Glen is that we knew he would make it back. The toughest thing was to replace him because he was playing some great footy in those years. Replacing Glen is tough now, but it was even more difficult then.

"Pace wasn't a big thing in Glen's game because he read the game so well and was able to adapt to each opponent. But it did have an influence on the team, probably more than we realised, until he came back to his best. Another 12 months down the track, he was playing good footy again, in 1998."

Trevor Nisbett

"It was just devastating. It cut me down in the prime of my career. I was really asserting myself on the competition, but I wanted more team success and felt we had the side to do it. I wanted to continue doing all of that and football, being my source of life so to speak, my source of oxygen, was suddenly cut off. I couldn't comprehend how I would go about the recovery. It was a whole new experience for me.

"That was tough, but there wasn't a lot I could do. I started my rehabilitation almost straight away and just tried to support the guys as much as I could. There wasn't a lot I could do in that situation, other than to just be around the place. I spent a little time in the coaches' box. I asked to do that just so I could experience what the coaches went through.

"Woosha was in there at the same time. He did his knee in Round Two and it helped to have him around because we did our rehab. together. His progress was a good guide for me – he was a bit of guinea pig because, when Woosha did his knee, it was the first one at the club since Dean Laidley. Medical science had come a little way since Dean's injury and we had gone some time since experiencing one. All of a sudden, we had three or four blokes

---

While Mary saw the rise of her son to be one of the great players of his time, she also saw Glen at his lowest ebb – when he suffered a serious knee injury in 1996.

"When Glen did his knee, that was a nightmare," she said. "He couldn't accept it and they (the media) were all hiding in the trees waiting for him. That was bad. I was at that game and I don't know how I got home. I went down to the rooms and spoke to the doctor. Glen hadn't come out at that stage and the doctor said to me, 'Mary, you have to be very patient with him, he won't accept it.' I don't know how I got home, I cried all the way because I knew how much it meant to him.

"When I got home, he was on the carpet with Peter Sumich playing cards. He still reckoned there was nothing wrong with him, but I knew better. The next day when they told him, he was angry. In those days, if Glen was home, it wouldn't matter who was playing on the television, he and I would watch the game together. I didn't know what to do the next Saturday, the Dockers were playing, so I put it on. He just turned it over. He watched it for 15 minutes and then turned it over.

"Once the Eagles started taking him to some of the away games, he got a bit better. But he was devastated by that and it took a long while for him to come to terms with it."

Mary Jakovich

go down with them, as Brendon Fewster, a new player at the club, had done a knee, as did Chris Waterman. Muddy had an anterior cruciate ligament injury, but he didn't tear it. He was close to having the same result that we did but, without tearing it, he was managed through it and played about 11 more games that season.

"In other years, we could have been accused of wasting an opportunity, but in 1996 a few injuries took their toll. We won 11 straight through the middle of the year and had seen the emergence of Ben Cousins and Chad Morrison as well as Andrew Donnelly, who won the rookie of the year award, so we had a few players who stood up. Drew Banfield had a magnificent year; Phil Matera and David Wirrpunda made their debuts and Mick re-signed, so I felt we could have had another crack at the title but, with myself and John going down, it did leave a hole.

"We beat Carlton in Perth in the first elimination final and went to Melbourne to play Essendon. That was when the controversy started over finals. We won our first final, finished higher than the Bombers, who lost their first final, but we still had to play them on their turf. Any chance we had was lost when we had to travel in the second week of the finals.

That was when Kevin Sheedy appealed to all Victorian supporters to get to the game... there was nothing else going on in Melbourne and there were 86,000 people there; obviously most of them were barracking for Essendon.

"They got on a bit of a roll and belted us by about 14 goals. I was sitting in the stands with Woosha and it was quite depressing."

Rehab reality check

AS AN ELITE athlete, AFL footballers often lose touch with reality. For Glen Jakovich, the recovery process from a knee reconstruction provided him with an insight into how most people live their lives. His rehabilitation programme was conducted at the Selby Street Rehabilitation Centre, in Shenton Park, along with many other people who had suffered injuries in their everyday lives.

"After surgery, I had a lot of waste in my leg and it was just a matter of building up the muscles and strengthening my leg first," he said. "The new ligament needs time to settle down and re-grow. At one point in time, they weaken and you have to be careful through that period with your training so as not to put it under any undue duress.

"I did a lot of my rehab at Selby Street, and I did it with public people, which was quite good for me. Nowadays, they do the recovery at the club, within the inner sanctum, but I did mine at Selby Street and it was an experience for me, working alongside normal every day people – car crash victims, occupational health and safety casualties from the work force, people falling off roofs, a roof carpenter smashing his Achilles – so rocking up there on my first day, wondering why this had happened to me, it wasn't fair... it was a real eye opener.

"The reality was I would play football just under 11 months later and was paid well to do it. There was one lady at Selby Street who was a hit-and-run accident victim with a stolen car at a shopping centre – she had been there for two years and still wasn't able to run. She had both femurs snapped, she had more metal objects in her body than you could possibly imagine. We all had different goals – her goal was just to have quality of life and that really brought the perspective back for me.

"That motivated me there and then. The prognosis for me was that within 12 months I would be playing football again; just a year between the injury and having the knee rebuilt and being back out there. That was a big turning point in my life as a person. I was on a modified programme at the start of the pre-season, but it was improving all the time. Every four weeks we were measuring my leg to see if I had put any bulk or muscle on or whether it had deteriorated. A half-a-centimetre improvement was a big step and every month my goal was to have it improve a little bit. That was all part of the build up of returning to play.

"We had pencilled in Round Five or Six to play in 1997 and that was what I was directing all my energy towards. I just went about getting my knee right. One day I was sitting in the hospital and Brian Cook came to see me; he said that out of this negative could come a lot of positives. I thought he was joking, my leg was in a cast and was sitting in a sling above the bed; how could anything positive come from that?

"I had the commissioner of Worksafe WA at the time, Neil Bartholomaeus, contact me. He wanted to use me as an ambassador for Worksafe WA and for Occupational Health and Safety, basically because I had suffered an injury at my work place... he wanted to use that as an example. Because of my high profile and the high profile of the injury, he saw a chance to raise community awareness about work place safety. Seven years later, I'm still working for them and they have been very, very good to me. It has opened up some business doors and avenues for me.

"So the knee injury turned into something positive from a commercial sense as well as broadening my horizons and introducing me to a lot of people in the corporate world."

1997: colossal return

BY THE TIME Glen Jakovich took the field for the Round Six fixture against the Western Bulldogs in 1997, he was already a veteran of more than 100 matches and was a three-time club champion. Yet he felt like a rookie just embarking on an AFL career. There was a clear divide between his career before a knee reconstruction and that which began on that night against the Bulldogs at the WACA ground.

While youngsters just embarking on life in elite football are shrouded by doubts over their ability to cut it with the best, most of the reservations about Jakovich's comeback campaign came from outside sources rather than within. After all, Jakovich had been one of the premier defenders in the AFL for more than six seasons so he knew he was capable of performing at the level.

The doubters wondered whether Jakovich would struggle to regain the mobility required to play at centre half-back, the position he had made his own in one of the most dominant outfits ever seen in the AFL. It took only one game for Jakovich to silence those doubters, settling into AFL football like he had never been absent.

After the knee injury, many people considered Jakovich would struggle to make it back. Those within the inner sanctum of the club, however, were always confident he would return as a powerful force.

"People who wrote him off didn't know him very well," said West Coast Eagles Chief Executive Trevor Nisbett. He also had a serious ankle injury which required a few operations, as well as his shoulder problems and his knee. He is not the sort of person who gives up. It would worry him what people said, but it wouldn't worry him to the extent that he would throw in the towel. He has never done that from the time he was a young boy to when he came here.

"Everything has revolved around hard work and he has trained hard to get to where he is. He has always trained hard, he has always done it, he loves the training and he loves the involvement, that's why he's a champion. His commitment to get himself right was always first class – the more people knocked him, the harder he would try."

Trevor Nisbett

"The build up to my return was pretty big," he said. "I sat down with the orthopaedic surgeons and planned my return, settling on Round Six as the date. I was starting to feel pretty good and wanted to play in the Derby which I think was Round Three, but we decided to stick with Round Six. Woosha made it back for the Derby and I returned against the Bulldogs at the WACA.

"I picked it up pretty well straight away; once you get back into the motion of playing footy, instinct takes over, but there is always an element of doubt in your mind. There was so much publicity about David Schwarz and a few other players who came back early. He came back after 16 weeks, but I was confident I had done the correct rehabilitation and that my knee would hold up. We had a great team with the orthopaedic surgeons, physio Chris Barrett, Bill Sutherland (head trainer) and doctors Ken Fitch and Rod Moore, that we bounced ideas off each other because we wanted to make sure nothing happened again.

"I knew I had done the work, it was 10.5 months to the day that I played again; it was a long time... now they say that after eight months you are ready to play competitive sport again. The technology has developed so much, the leg was strong, I was fit and I'd virtually had a year off, so I was fit and ready to go. The last hurdle was twisting, turning, getting someone to knock you over, bumping you, taking your feet out from under you and not worrying where your knee was all the time. It is hard to simulate game conditions, but that was the final hurdle which I knew could take up to two years. For me, it did take a while, although I came back and played pretty well first-up. I think that was probably more to do with the emotion of the occasion... I was a bit inconsistent after that but, in the next six months, I played some of the best football of my career.

"There was a perception in the media that I would not be the same again; being a big bloke and suffering a knee injury, they rarely come back to emulate feats achieved before the injury. That was already weighing heavily on my mind and I thought 'well hang on, give me a chance to prove it.' After that game against the Bulldogs, I played the two finals and won the player of the finals award. I played 16 games that year and injured my other knee, which caused me to miss three games with a medial ligament strain.

"So I had my fair share of setbacks, but I still ended up playing close to a full season of football... I played some really good footy as well as some games where I was a bit apprehensive, particularly on the shifting surface of the Melbourne grounds. I slipped over a few times and that created some doubts. The biggest hurdle was psychological, just the fact that I might do it again. I wore a brace that maintained the heat in my knee. It made sure the blood was flowing and circulating so that it was never cold, which was the most important thing. Sometimes, if they're a bit cold, you can do some unnecessary damage. It's like warming up and stretching if you have done a hamstring or a quad. If the muscles around the knee are not contracting, then all ligaments become vulnerable. Because I had a new graft in my knee, I couldn't afford for that to happen.

"Coming to terms with the injury took time. For a bigger bloke it takes longer – in all, it took me two years to regain absolute confidence. In 1998 I played all the games, but then had a severe ankle injury on the other foot. I just went through a period where I had a few injuries, from the knee to the other knee, to my ankle, to bone spurs and three or four operations.

"Mentally I wasn't strong enough to convince myself I was ready to go. I went through some self-doubt but, once I got over that, my next two years were really good. In 1999 and 2000 I finished high up in the fairest and best in one year and won it in the other. The self-doubts were something I had never confronted before and I dealt with it by myself.

"I spoke to a lot of people, I spoke to Tim Watson who came back from a knee injury to win two fairest and best awards, and technology is more advanced now than it was back then. I spoke with Doug Hawkins – he actually has a synthetic ligament in his knee which has a 90 percent failure rate, a procedure which is used in the US with a lot of the grid iron players. Because he's a smaller type player, I suppose he could get away with it.

"I got so used to playing footy, week in, week out; over four years I didn't miss a game, (so) that I was going from one extreme to the other. Having to undergo a knee reconstruction changed the whole complexion of my career. It's not an injury where you can have plenty of rest for the first couple of weeks, then start some rehabilitation and pick up where you left off. It was the end of one phase of my career and the beginning of a new one.

"It took a little while to work through that. It was a challenge to see whether I could come back and achieve the heights I did earlier and I did that. It was very character-building and I steeled myself through the experience. It is not an experience I would recommend to anyone else, but I was better for it."

One of the downs that came in Jakovich's resumption was against his old foe Wayne Carey, when the North Melbourne champion scored a decisive victory against his arch rival; this again ignited the embers of doubt. Rarely had Jakovich been so comprehensively beaten.

"Carey stitched me right up at Subiaco Oval," he said. "The media had already started to get into me, questioning whether I could get back and that time had passed me by. I was only 25 years of age and I was thinking I had plenty to offer.

"Everyone seemed to be sinking the boots into me and I knew I had to just wear that, bide my time and move forward. I played reasonably well for the rest of the year and then started my campaign of proving to myself that I could play good footy. I had to prove to myself that I could play on the best players in the competition again, which I was able to do. It was also pay-back time when I came up against a few opponents.

"The club was very supportive. Mick said I was still in the team's best 18, that I was the best centre half-back in the competition and I just had to work at it. He said it was up to me to get over the adversity. I set high standards and was playing okay games, but not to the standard I had set previously in my career. From that side of things I could understand where people were coming from to a certain extent.

"I always cast my mind back to when my father died at a young age and I was able to contend with that. I worked through it with my family and figured if I could do that, I could get through anything. Experiencing the death of someone close to you at a vulnerable age leaves you no alternative but to go forward. There were people in the media taking pot shots at me, I had to sit back and absorb it and work my way through it. I used to talk to myself to get through training sessions and games and just try to put in a performance that would start to turn things around. I had to find an opening and, sure enough, the openings came and I was ready. I had the ambition, the vigour and the motivation to come back."

In years from now, when football aficionados debate the virtues of Glen Jakovich, they will undoubtedly mention one other name to support their view – Wayne Carey. At a time when individual rivalries have diminished because players need to be flexible to operate in different areas of the ground, the Jakovich-Carey battles were always a wonderful aside to West Coast-North Melbourne (Kangaroos) contests.

West Coast chief executive Trevor Nisbett witnessed all of those show downs and was as enthralled as anyone.

"You had the best centre half-forward for so many years against the best centre half-back for so many years," Nisbett enthused. "I don't think there is any doubt about that and Jakovich-Carey clashes will go down in history as the match-up of the '90s.

"I don't think I got too engrossed in it until I watched the replays and saw the quality of play between the two of them. Some of the games in the mid to late '90s were such unbelievable matches, but the strange thing was that, if Wayne got on top of Glen, the Kangaroos didn't necessarily win the game. Wayne kicked five goals a couple of times on Glen, but they didn't win. I think everyone else was doing their job and vice versa. If Glen blanketed Carey, we didn't necessarily win the game, but it was such an individual match-up and contest, it was quite unbelievable at times.

"The head-to-head battle would be marginal overall. From a biased point of view, we would say Glen was in front. If Glen had any weakness in his game, it was probably that the lesser lights got under his guard. He was very good on a good player, while some of the lesser opponents could get under his guard when he wasn't concentrating at his best."

Trevor Nisbett

1998: Woosha's sad farewell

IN THE CAREER of Glen Jakovich, it is doubtful whether there was a more controversial on-field development than the demise of popular skipper John Worsfold, who had led the club through a remarkable era and was a man who embodied everything for which the West Coast Eagles stood. If a fairytale finish were possible, it would have ended with another premiership. In reality, it could not have concluded in greater contrast.

As the team prepared for a 1998 final against the Western Bulldogs, Worsfold tried everything to prove his fitness, but the match committee was not convinced. And, on the eve of the game, the decision was made to leave a battle weary Worsfold out of the team. As teammates prepared for the contest at the MCG, it became clear that their highly respected skipper would not be playing. A few of Worsfold's close confidantes had been told, but the rest discovered his omission just hours before the match.

"The player group should have been told three or four days before... John Worsfold was going on the bus to the game with his footy bag," Jakovich said. "We were 10 minutes away from playing and Woosha was still in his tracksuit. We were shell-shocked. We were never a chance anyway and it was just tragic. We thought 'well, what are we doing here?' You could just see the impact it had on the whole player group.

"I roomed with Woosha the night before so I had some inclination because he basically said he wasn't playing. He had been asked to drop himself – he said he wasn't going to do that because he had done everything he could to get himself right and felt he could offer something out there. Mick said he wasn't going to drop John Worsfold, it was up to John to make that call. I don't know what happened from that time to the start of the game, but the night before we were playing cards and having a chat about it.

"Once I got to the game, because I was so focused on getting prepared for a cut-throat final, I didn't have time to deal with it. I ran out and had to lead the side because Bluey (McKenna) was injured and didn't make the trip and Woosh was left out. In the end, I locked it out and pushed it to one side because I had an important final to play. I had to block it out because I had a responsibility to play a game of football, but perhaps some of my younger teammates couldn't do that.

"I thought it was poorly handled at the time – they should have reached a decision earlier in the week; they must have had an inclination as to whether John could play or not.

"From what I hear, the medical staff said John was in no physical condition to play. Still, to this day, I don't know what happened between Mick, the doctors, John and the match committee. In the end, John Worsfold should have played. It was always going to be his last year and that would have been his last game. We wouldn't have won even if John had played, but at least he would have been given the honour of leading his side for the last time. Instead, he had to sit in the box and watch his teammates get belted. No-one was more gut-wrenched than John, it was like someone had reached in and ripped his heart out.

"Everyone makes mistakes and I don't think that should be held against Mick forever and a day. The match committee made a mistake and I think they are sorry about it, although I don't know whether Mick has ever said that. I think he's sorry for the event. It's only a small thing now in John's past, he's moved on. After the game, I was shattered that we lost... then there was the media and everything else going on in the rooms. It was a frenzy. Our dynasty was over and it was a matter of starting again."

1999: end of an era

Rather than being the end of his problems, the knee reconstruction proved to be the beginning. As so often happens with players resuming from a serious knee injury, trouble flares in other parts of the body – Jakovich was no exception.

"In 1999 I had a good start, but then had a little setback with an ankle injury where I needed surgery and missed a week," Jakovich said. "That took another month to get over and my form was there-abouts. Then I hit a purple patch in the middle of the year and ended up finishing in the top five in the fairest and best. We won a final and lost a final. When I look back on the year, I played every game bar one, finished top five in the fairest and best and, had it not been for that injury, which set me back a month, I could easily have been right up there at the top again.

"I knew that I'd laid the foundation to move forward and felt that was the end of any on-going concerns with the knee injury. I stopped wearing the brace; it had been three years since I had done it and I was ready to move on. I played pretty well in the finals that year. In the first game I played on Chris Grant on a blustery night, which was a tough assignment, and I knew when I'd got to the end of that game that I had beaten it.

"I sat down with Mick, who was obviously going to Collingwood at that stage, and he said to me 'you're there. You're obviously growing in confidence, you had a good year, you're a proven performer again, played well in the big games, you don't face any post-season surgery, embrace the new system and the new coach (Ken Judge).'"

The end of the 1999 season saw Malthouse move on, amid claims that he had not focused totally on his role with West Coast. Jakovich will have none of that.

"I can't understand people saying Mick didn't coach with the same intensity towards the end of 1999 because he had made the decision to go to Collingwood," Jakovich said of his long-time mentor. "You only had to look at that second-last game against Footscray when we won by two points. He was jumping up and down in the coaches' box, his headset fell off, he was over the moon. I never sensed any change in Mick. He probably knew himself that he was going, but Mick was always a bloke that if he had a job to do, he saw it through.

"He didn't bail out on us at any stage. We were still a silly chance for the finals, but obviously our away form in the second half of the season was struggling. We finished fifth at the end of the year and Mick's time was up. In the last 10 weeks he was coaching with just as much enthusiasm and passion as he had done at any stage of his career. At the time, I was disappointed he left but, looking back, I suppose his time had come. I think it was time for him to move on. Having said that, we missed the finals in 2000 and, if he had stayed, I reckon we would have made it again because he was able to get things out of players that others couldn't. Mick could have gotten something extra out of the group. He was fantastic over a long period of time. The times we had were so good, but all good things come to an end.

"I remember sitting at the club champion awards at the end of 1999 when Mick made his final address which was quite emotional. He was a man who came over from Melbourne and changed the face of the club from a playing perspective promote a professional attitude, a high level of discipline and a high level of intensity for training, for every minute of the day that you're involved in football. He was so passionate about getting the best out of every individual so they could get the best out of themselves.

"He set that culture within the club. People tell me, because he was the only coach I knew in the first nine years at the West Coast Eagles, that there was an entirely different culture at the club when he arrived to when he left. He installed a high level of discipline and worked us hard as a player group. We all know that he had a very good player group when he arrived and he turned a lot of us into dual premiership players. Players embraced that, respected him for that. There were a few things along the way that didn't go down all that well which are well documented, like the parting of John Worsfold and Chris Mainwaring. I think it's fair to say that if Mick had his time over again he would have handled those things better. I think, in the end, every club has its hiccups and, in time, everyone moves on and it's forgotten and forgiven."

Mick's mark

MOST football enthusiasts in WA have an opinion on the impact that Mick Malthouse had in a decade at the helm of the State's premier football club – he produced the first team outside of Melbourne to claim the VFL/AFL premiership. His detractors say he had virtually a State team to work with. But, regardless of the talent at his disposal – and there was no doubt an abundance of it – the coach still had to impose himself on the group and mould them into a unit capable of claiming the game's ultimate prize.

Certainly Glen Jakovich holds Malthouse in the highest esteem and credits both individual and team success on his mentor's ability to transform a skilful running team into the most feared combination in the country.

"Mick taught us what a method of football was all about," Jakovich says. "Over here in the West you get so caught up in your own fishbowl about how great we are, but he knew we needed to change things if we were going to win a flag. That's why we needed a hard-nosed Victorian coach. One thing people don't understand is that Mick is a very compassionate man, he actually would find out about every person's life, the strengths they have, the weaknesses they have, where they come from, the events that have shaped their lives.

"He likes to find inspiration within his own player group, whether one of his players jumped in front of a speeding car to save a small child, that sort of thing. He would draw on that to bring the player group together. He was very strong in those areas. Mick's a family man, his family is very, very important to him.

"He was very emotional and that shone through in his last game. The press conference after his last game as coach of West Coast was packed in the old Richmond rooms. I remember the journalists putting down their microphones, pens and paper and giving Mick a standing ovation. I had never been at a press conference before when the journos did that. He had Bluey on one side, me on the other and we spoke about the journey, the 10 years, the premierships, the players."

2000-2001: changing of the guard

AFTER an unprecedented run of success, playing finals football in every year of the 1990s decade, there was a major shift in the infrastructure of the West Coast Eagles. The most notable change in personnel was the return of Mick Malthouse to Melbourne to coach Collingwood and the appointment of Ken Judge as his successor.

Judge, who coached East Fremantle to premierships in 1992 and 1994, was an assistant coach to David Parkin at Carlton in 1995 and then coached Hawthorn for four years. He seemed to have the best credentials to succeed but, after two barren years at the helm, when the club finished 13th and 14th, Judge was sacked. He had lost the support of the board and, according to Glen Jakovich, the players. Had Judge not been replaced, Jakovich estimates that up to 15 players would have sought out a trade to another club or would have nominated for the draft.

"He changed a little in the second year because so much focus and pressure went on to him," Jakovich said of the man who coached the club in 2000 and 2001. "From about Round Six or Seven, the pressure started to go on him. My form was just okay, but the team started to lose and when we lost we came under some scrutiny. I could see Ken starting to have doubts about himself. We were all in survival mode. Ken was coaching for survival, I was playing for survival. The team wasn't going crash hot and we were being belted on average by about 11 goals.

"It was a very tough period. That was when I realised you really had to cherish the good times and understand that, throughout your career, you are going to have your peaks and troughs. For me, it was like going to Mt Everest at the start of my career and then crashing down to the base of the mountain. Not making the finals for the first time in my career certainly tested the club's character. What we did in the space of 12 months, when Woosha replaced Ken, takes some clubs three years to recover from, to claw out of that rut. We had two years with Ken and they came and went quickly in the end.

"With the same player group, plus Chris Judd, we made the finals the next year. It was a tough time but, with the people the club has around the place like Trevor Nisbett, the board and just the whole infrastructure, it is designed not to accept failure. Players were talking about Judgey's future. Some were saying they couldn't wait until the end of the year to find out what was going on. It was either him or them; many were either going to ask to be traded or put themselves into the draft.

"There were players who had fallen out with Ken because he put no confidence in them. Ken was quite brutal in some of his messages to the players, a lot of it borne out of the frustration of where we were at; we were in a rut, getting belted and he wanted to find a way out. I guess it was frustrating when the players didn't give him their support, which was quite evident. He had my support because I tried to build that relationship, but I felt his biggest downfall was a lack of communication to the whole player group.

"That came mainly in the second year – my relationship with him also dwindled at the same time, I suppose because the focus was so much on him. When he first arrived it was different. We got off to a good start, he communicated with all the players and brought some good initiatives and ideas to the playing group, but then he tried to change the culture of the club. Whether it was the Hawthorn way or trying to get out of the Malthouse mentality, I'm not sure. I always felt that whoever replaced Mick Malthouse was going to have one helluva job because Mick was right up there at the top of his profession.

"When Judgey came in he tried to get us to embrace a different way of playing our football, which, in the end, cost him his job and probably his coaching career. Players weren't surprised when the announcement came that he had been dismissed. A lot of players were relieved. A number felt they would like to stay in Perth because it's a good place and a great club and the facilities are fantastic, but they just didn't get on with the coach. So they looked out for other opportunities. I reckon 15 players might have left, a mix of young and experienced guys."

To have more than a third of the playing group looking at alternatives certainly made for an unstable environment and it's little wonder the team fell to some demoralising defeats, particularly against Carlton and Hawthorn, at Optus Oval and the MCG respectively.

When Judge initially assumed control, many players welcomed the change. At the same time, the club shifted location at Subiaco Oval, moving diagonally from the half-forward flank on the railway line side of the ground to the pocket facing Roberts Road at the city end of the stadium into a $5-million development. The new headquarters included an expansive administration section, a swimming pool, a gymnasium, a rehabilitation room, lecture theatre, coaches' offices, medical rooms and a special players' lounge, making the facility second-to-none in the league. In all, it made for a totally fresh start for all concerned and, initially, everything was rosy. For senior players like Jakovich, Dean Kemp, Chris Lewis, Ashley McIntosh, Peter Matera and Guy McKenna, who had played almost exclusively under Malthouse, it was a total sea change.

Immediately upon his appointment, Judge spoke of the club being at the crossroads, obviously referring to that senior group who he considered to be on the downward spiral towards the end of their careers. Jakovich, 27 at the time, considered his classification as a fading star to be premature, so he sought out Judge for an explanation.

"It was a whole new experience for me going into a season with a different coach," says Jakovich. "I was going into my 27th year, so I was at the back end of my career and it was quite critical for me – if the new coach didn't like me, I'd be in trouble.

"The perception straight away with Ken was that the club was on a knife's edge; at the crossroads. He thought we had so many great players heading towards the end of their careers that we might have to replace them and go through this rebuilding phase. Unfortunately, he put me on that side of the fence with the ageing players. What some people had failed to remember was that, while I played in those premierships with players like Michael Brennan, John Worsfold, Chris Lewis, Peter Wilson, Dean Kemp, Guy McKenna and Chris Mainwaring, I was four or five years younger than most of them.

"I was still a relatively young man and felt I had a lot of football left in me. So there were a few teething issues, but I confronted Ken in much the same way that I had faced Mick a decade earlier. I told Ken I was passionate about my footy, I was loyal to the club and to him and I was willing to do anything he asked of me. He embraced that straight away and we got off to a good start. Looking back now, I don't think too many players had a good working relationship with Ken. I was one of a few who did and felt that was because of my experience, seniority and knowledge, and that I broke the ground early by having an interview with him.

"Basically, I made him aware of what my goals and visions were so that he could understand what I was trying to achieve through my career and he could put that into the game plan and we could all benefit. I think he appreciated that. He had one perception of me and straight away I was able to change that, which helped me and enabled him to have faith in me. There were a couple of times where we came to a notch in the road and he backed me. I didn't let him down and I can't be sure, but I think that if I hadn't made those early approaches to him, he might not have backed me and could have taken the attitude that my time was up and it was right to go with the youth."

That chat with the coaching incumbent, combined with a strong finals performance against Footscray in 1999, seemed to help the initial relationship between Judge and one of his senior players.

"My form in 1999 was good and Judgey knew when he was watching the finals series that he was coming to the Eagles and I'd played well," Jakovich says. "He mentioned that to me in the first interview – he said my performance on Chris Grant was sensational and had been instrumental in the team achieving victory, so that was all positive. I got off to a good start with Ken, which was encouraging. I believe it's every player's responsibility to approach the match committee and the coach to find out where they fit in the plans.

"We started the Judge reign with a bang and smashed the Kangaroos at the MCG under lights on a night when they unfurled their premiership flag. We were confident of going well, we played really well and beat them impressively. Then there were thumping wins over Adelaide and Fremantle, when Scott Cummings kicked 14 and 10 goals respectively and we were fifth after Round Seven... but it was all downhill from there on. We dropped 10 of the last 11 matches and completely lost our way. It was all new ground; we had a number of injuries and lost Michael Gardiner to a shoulder and Ben Cousins to an ankle.

"Some players just weren't playing up to AFL standard and were traded after that. We had some great players retiring and others moving on and there were a whole lot of things happening that year. We had to clean the slate and start over again."

That Derby

Since the very first Western Derby, there have been some wonderful clashes between the two clubs, the most memorable in Round 22 of the 2000 season when Fremantle won a spiteful battle by a solitary behind on a day which opened with a sparring duel between Eagles ruckman Michael Gardiner and young Docker Matthew Pavlich. That set the tone for a physical confrontation which saw some old fashioned hay-makers thrown and resulted in a nine match suspension for Fremantle journeyman Dale Kickett.

While many spectators were surprised at the physical nature of the contest, a throw-back to the 1980s if you like, the West Coast Eagles players had anticipated such a confrontation. Word on the street was that Fremantle was anxious to make a stand, having been brushed aside quite easily in some previous encounters.

"The Derby which really stuck in my mind was the one they won by a point," Glen Jakovich revealed. "The one with all the fights, the lead changed a number of times during the game and they got us. That really changed the course of the Derbies. That was basically them standing up and saying they weren't going to bow to us any more. We all believed it was premeditated and that Damian Drum went out and told his players to throw cut lunches.

"If that was their tactic then I disagree with it, but it worked for them, they got the four points. They stood up and earned a bit of respect. They didn't just go out and have a bit of a punch-up, they played well enough to win the game of football. I didn't respect them entirely for the way they went about it, but they earned some admiration because they weren't going to have sand kicked in their face any more. There was probably a better way to do it and there were a few cheap shots taken in the game. The AFL dealt with it harshly and they needed to.

"Players involved in those blues were either heavily suspended or fined and the AFL had to take a tough stance. Dale Kickett got nine weeks. That's half a year of football and you have to wonder whether it was the right thing to do. To follow the coach's directions, but to then miss half a season of football as a consequence – you have to wonder whether that's the right way to play footy."

Captaincy let down

WHEN brilliant defender Guy McKenna was forced into retirement because of a persistent back injury at the end of the 1999 season, it presented an interesting poser for the club. McKenna, who had assumed the captaincy on the retirement of John Worsfold, ended his reign after a club record 267 games, but there was no obvious replacement as skipper.

Would new coach Ken Judge recommend young gun Ben Cousins as skipper? Or would he go with one of the senior players who might not necessarily be there to guide the club through to its next triumph? In that case, would it be Peter Matera, Jakovich or Dean Kemp, who had been something of a reluctant leader in the past. Much of the pre-season football debate centred around the issue, but Judge and his match committee justifiably wanted to assess the claims of all candidates during the pre-season. It proved a difficult time, not just for the match committee, but for the players involved as well.

"When the captaincy became available it was a real tough time," Jakovich recalls. "I had re-signed with the club and we couldn't talk about the captaincy because it was going to be announced at a CUB launch, as part of new $30-million sponsorship announcement at a gala affair on Subiaco Oval.

"They were going to announce the team leaders at both West Coast and Fremantle and, between the end of the season and February 7, when this launch was scheduled, there was so much speculation about the captaincy... they had telephone polls, they had television polls, they had radio polls. It just became so overwhelming. They generally had me as the leading candidate, but at the time I knew I wasn't getting the job because I felt they would have told me and asked me to keep it quiet.

"In the end they went with the dual captaincy with Cuzzy and Dean Kemp. I couldn't understand why they went for the dual captaincy because I was younger than Kempy. I've always admired Kempy, the way he played the game and how he led from the front, so I could understand why he was a leader. But, given that age was one of the reasons why they didn't go for me, was a little perplexing.

"It was just another issue I had to work through and, at the end of the day, I was still going to play footy. It wasn't as if I had another knee injury. At the time it was disappointing because I was always touted as a future captain and I had set my sights on doing that – I wanted to lead the club and the team.

"In the end when I woke up the next morning, knowing I didn't get the gig, I thought 'all that heartache for nothing.' I could move on then, go to training and get ready to play footy. I was more than happy once the result had been delivered to move on with my life and my season. It didn't mean I wouldn't lead because I was one of a couple of vice-captains. So that didn't bother me."

Busted ankle, broken pride

THE COMPETITIVE juices run strong through the Glen Jakovich veins; occasionally to his own detriment, such as the time in the 2001 pre-season when he played in a social match at Waroona, in WA's South-West. The first bad decision was to play the match. The second was to throw himself recklessly into the fray, resulting in a serious injury as he committed himself to take a spectacular boundary-line catch. He severely damaged his ankle and almost impaled himself on the picket fence which bordered the quaint little ground. That incident had terrible ramifications for that season and cast serious doubt over his playing future.

"If I hadn't broken my ankle in that charity cricket match I reckon I could have enjoyed a good year because I was really prepared and fully fit," Jakovich said. "I actually pulled out of the cricket match the day before, but Ken Judge begged me to play because he had been involved in the organisation.

"I missed four months of crucial pre-season training as a result. Brad Bootsma, who was playing for Fremantle at the time, was batting and it was a mixed team of Fremantle and Eagles players, a few celebrities and some cricketers like Ian Chappell, Kim Hughes and Bruce Yardley. Bootsma and I went to school together, so I knew him quite well. He was a very good cricketer and, in the previous over, he had carted me over the fence a couple of times and I was pretty sour. After my over, I went down to third man and he sent a catch my way. I thought 'I'm going to catch this' and kept running with my eye on the ball. I ran into the fence and did a real number on myself. I almost impaled myself on the fence. I'd never broken a bone in my life, with all the footy I've played. But, in this social cricket match, I broke the tailis at the front of my ankle, missed four months of pre-season and just got up for the start of the year. I played every game that season, but went from winning the fairest and best to not finishing top 10, which meant I went from one extreme to the other."

"The cricket accident was really disappointing and, while a lot of people would say he shouldn't have been taking part, he was playing with the football coach of the time," West Coast Eagles Chief Executive Trevor Nisbett said. "It was a friendly and, again, he was his own worst enemy because his commitment to everything he does is full bore. His competitiveness wrecked his ankle and consequently he was in real trouble because if you can't run, you can't play league footy. But he worked his way through that as well. Again, a lot of people wrote him off, but he was always going to get back. He has always been trying to maintain his pace and strength. Eventually, time catches up with you, but certainly no-one has been more diligent than Glen Jakovich in terms of getting his body right and staying away from alcohol and drugs which come into people's lives these days."

Trevor Nisbett

2002: Woosha returns

AFTER the dismissal of Ken Judge as senior coach at the end of the 2001 season, there was much speculation as to who would be his replacement. A number of contenders were thrown forward by the media, including premiership captain John Worsfold, Adelaide assistant Neil Craig and Hawthorn assistant Chris Connolly. For a few weeks, when speculation was at its peak, many of the West Coast Eagles players were kicking back in Bali. The 2001 season had been arduous; the players had not lived up to expectations and they felt some responsibility for the coach's demise. But after Judge had parted company, it was a matter of looking ahead – Jakovich says the players were ecstatic when Worsfold, who had spent two years as an assistant coach at Carlton, was appointed.

"We were elated that Woosha got the job," Jakovich said. "Some major steps were in place after a poor season and Ken Judge got the sack. There was an eight week period between Ken's dismissal and when John was appointed and that was basically the players' eight week rest. We had a football trip to Bali and there was a fair amount of resolve from the guys, having lost 10 of our last 11 games, with an average losing margin of 11 goals. We got together and said this isn't much fun and we need to do something about it.

"Ken got the sack as head coach and, while a number of candidates were thrown around, we didn't think too much about it because it was out of our control. But, on the trip, we got together and worked on ourselves about how we were going to get out of this rut and start to rebuild the club. The cream on the cake was the appointment of John Worsfold because a lot of the guys playing at the time had played with him and we knew what Woosha was like. It was a new era about to start under the John Worsfold regime.

"Basically, his first year was a suck-and-see-it exercise, but he was heavily involved in promoting professionalism. Just the simple things in a footy club. He cleaned out a few players – basically John's biggest thing was professionalism. Everyone was committed to making the football club great again and he questioned a few people on their character – he asked what they were doing outside of football, to mingle a bit more with the community outside of football and not lock themselves away from everyday people. He thought that would help the guys realise they had a unique opportunity and shouldn't take it for granted."

After Worsfold had retired as a player and before he moved to Carlton, he spent a year in Perth working in the media and assessing his options – Jakovich remained in close contact. The players were officially drawing the curtain on a poor 2001 season when Jakovich called his former skipper. The annual post-season wake was in full swing when Jakovich made the call.

"I spoke to Woosh when the job was still up in the air and basically asked him, at our wake at Steve's Hotel, whether he was in with a chance," Jakovich said. "He thought he would get one of the two jobs in WA because he had applied for the Fremantle post as well.

"There and then, at the lowest point of our careers, especially for myself, I just thought Woosha would help me if he was appointed because he knew who I was and what I stood for. I was worried about a new coach coming in and, looking at the list, at blokes like myself, Ashley McIntosh, Roo (Matera), and saying 'they were great players, but it's about time we drew a line in the sand and said it's time to move them on.' We all felt we had something to offer the football club, given an opportunity and a pre-season and a bit of persistence.

"After John was appointed, we all had player interviews and he had all the stats from the year before, a bit of a review and an analysis of where each player was at and where to from here. I was a bit wary of how to approach it, but what turned my career around was that my interview went for about three minutes, John didn't want to talk about the past, didn't want to dwell on my poor year, he just basically said 'you're my No.1 centre half-back, I need you up and firing, just go and get yourself fit.' They were the most encouraging words and something I hadn't experienced for a couple of years. At 28 years of age, coming towards the twilight of my career, I walked out of there like someone with an injection of adrenaline into my body.

"A three minute meeting with Woosha was good for me and it was special. John was a good mate of mine and he backed me in and trusted me and I couldn't let him down. It was like the old days on the footy field when John would demand something and you couldn't let him down. But he would demand it, knowing that you could deliver. John's a professional and I have always conducted myself as a professional. I thought it would work for both of us. I'm not one for taking short cuts, I never have been and I was not about to use the power of our friendship to accommodate lack-lustre form or preferential selection in the side."

While the 2001 season had been one of personal and team lows, Jakovich was determined to reverse the trend.

"I just wanted to go through that year as well as I possibly could," he said. "The previous year I received some negative publicity, some of which was warranted and some that wasn't but, in any club that gets belted like we did, winning only five games, the critics and the fans are going to pick on areas they think need improvement.

"They looked at some of the proven premiership players and thought we'd had our time and it was time to move on. I thought I was harshly dealt with by some sections of the media. I thought 'I'm 28 years of age, I'm healthy, I'm fit, I'm strong, but I just had a poor season.' I also thought there were legitimate reasons for that poor season and it could be tracked back to that injury. I knew the reasons why and people like Trevor Nisbett and Tim Gepp were very supportive.

"The other advantage coming into 2002 was that I didn't need any post-season surgery, so I had my eight weeks off and just came straight back into pre-season. I felt good being around the place – the arrival of John was like a breath of fresh air around the club. The last three months under Ken were very, very difficult. I'm not blaming Ken or anything, but there was a lot of sniping going on, there were problems with the match committee and you could see the unrest within that group... it filtered through to the players. There was a lot of unrest and a club which had taken great pride in itself and its resilience was fragmenting.

"We were looking to achieve honourable losses. Instead of losing by 12 goals we lost by eight. When you know you're not going to win a game, you start to worry about yourself and how you're performing. It was totally unfamiliar territory for me because I had played in such a dynasty. We played a lot of finals footy and had a lot of success, but I benefited from the experience. When I look back, I've been to Mt Everest a couple of times and have been right down to the bottom. I was at the lowest ebb about Round 18, 2001 when we were really struggling and just waiting for the last four or five weeks of the season to end. The last four or five weeks felt like four or five months. To climb back up there, from a team point of view and from an individual point of view, has been great. We haven't climbed Mt Everest yet, but we're on our way and have taken some important steps forward.

"To play finals the following year, with basically the same list that finished third last and was considered by Robert Walls as having the worst list in the competition, was quite an achievement. Walls, a former Carlton premiership player and coach, tipped us to finish last in John's first year, but to finish eighth and play off in a finals series was a great learning experience for the club.

"It was a great experience for John and his new match committee and the realisation of what a bit of belief and confidence can do. We did that with the same list of players, plus the inclusion of Chris Judd, that was supposed to finish last."

Heart beat worries

IT WAS a mid-week training session and the level of excitement in the West Coast Eagles change rooms was higher than normal. There was frantic activity around the doctor's room as Glen Jakovich hoisted his training bag over his shoulder and shouted to Dr Rod Moore that he would see him at the hospital. Jakovich had felt a little out of kilter for a few days and, when he came off the training track, he casually asked Dr Moore to check his heart rate. The popular medico detected an irregular heart beat inside the massive chest.

The result triggered some alarm, particularly when Jakovich was left out of the travelling party to tackle St Kilda in Round 12, 2002. Initially it was thought the problem could be rectified swiftly, but soon it became apparent that no chances should be taken. Jakovich was left out of the team and a frenzy resulted within the local media when the reason for his absence was divulged. Anything relating to an irregular heartbeat is always going to generate some degree of hysteria but, for Jakovich himself, it was also alarming because there didn't seem to be a specific trigger.

"It is a little bit of a concern... it has happened four times now," Jakovich explained. "My cardiologist has put it down to the fact that it just happens and it's a little difficult to accept at times because you can't work out what it is. After the initial problem, it came back 12 months later and then again six months after that; there doesn't seem to be anything specific which triggers it. Then, in pre-season for 2004, it happened again.

"The cardiologist just reckons I have a lot of electricity in my body; I've always been a hyperactive fellow so that could have something to do with it. It's possible it has something to do with my diet, so I've cut a few things out. I can drink coffee, but not umpteen amounts of it. Apparently it's common in healthy young people. Training a lot causes my metabolism to move up and down rapidly.

"He got concerned about it because, as fast as I went out of rhythm, I got back into rhythm with a simple dose of medication, which was not a heavy drug. Within 72 hours, I was back into rhythm. If you don't get back into rhythm, you could face procedures which could prevent you playing football, or any physical activity at the highest level, but that doesn't seem to happen.

"It was scary the first time it happened. I was in St John of God's in the Intensive Care Unit, not because I needed to be there, but that was the only place they could hook me up to a heart monitor. They ran an ECG straight away and I was running at about 140 beats per minute, which was quite high for someone who had been off the track for a while.

"I had noticed something amiss at least three months before, about Round 11, but I remember feeling it in pre-season and just put it down to the hot weather, the heavy work load and I was perspiring a lot. I distinctly remember playing with that for the first 10 weeks, plus a few scratch matches, without recognising what it was. I was feeling very upbeat when going to bed and then, one day after training, I asked the doc to take my blood pressure. I thought my blood pressure was up and told him I felt a little up-tempo and wasn't relaxed. He took my resting pulse and he nearly fainted. He asked me how long I'd been off the track for and I said nearly an hour.

"I had showered and was ready to go home. I was just getting a bit of ice on my foot, from a kick received in training and he said we need you to go over to St John of God because your heart is out of rhythm. He was pretty calm, probably so it didn't set off panic stations with me. I met Dr Phillip Cook, the cardiologist, and he put me on the ECG and told me I had a heart fibrillation, which is a condition of the heart when it beats out of rhythm. The first time was quite easy because they gave me the medication. It didn't kick straight back into rhythm, but there is a procedure where they send a wire up one of the arteries through my leg to the bottom of the heart, which is a 10 minute procedure and it kicks the heart back into gear.

"It was quite ironic because Emely and the whole family on her side were in Adelaide for a wedding and my daughter was there as well, but Mum was home so Doc Moore rang her; she was okay when she heard my voice because I was quite calm. At that stage, I thought I'd be released within 20 minutes or half an hour and would be on a plane the next day to play St Kilda. I probably saw myself as bullet proof and then, all of a sudden, there is this condition which I can't control. I couldn't just have an ultrasound or get a trainer to rub it and fix it... I was in the hands of doctors, specialists.

"From the point of view that it was out of my control, it was a ghostly feeling. It was probably the first time in my life I was unable to control things and I felt uncomfortable. I was reassured by the doctors who said they could get it back to a regular beat within 48 hours and there was a 90 percent chance it wouldn't happen again. I had the procedure, took three days off and then came back and played the next week."

While there was a 90 percent chance it wouldn't recur, that meant there was a 10 percent chance that it would. And almost exactly 12 months later it did.

"The second time around it was a bit more depressing and I was thinking 'what's happening here,'" Jakovich said. "The second time was different because I knew on the Monday that I had it and I trained on the Tuesday, thought I'd just see how I went on the Wednesday. But then I knew it was out, so I went down and saw Dr Gerard Taylor, who put the stethoscope on my chest and said I was out of rhythm again.

"I knew that 48 hours beforehand, but I was hoping it might just kick back in naturally. You feel your heart racing; it does other things to your emotions as well and affects you

Replica Cup…Jakovich clings to a replica of the 1992 premiership cup.

West Coast Eagles training staff work on Jakovich's powerful legs during a break in action.

Gym junkie...Jakovich poses for a photo in the club gymnasium, where he sculptured his imposing frame.

An early milestone (above) and sharing a great moment with South Fremantle teammates Peter Sumich and David Hart in 1994.

All smiles…After the 1994 premiership triumph Jakovich shares a moment of celebration with Don Pyke, Chris Waterman and Peter Sumich.

Premiership glory is the motivation for playing and in 1994 he shared the success with Adrian Barich (above), Paul Symmons and wife Emely.

Darwin heat... Jakovich re-hydrates after an exhausting practice match in Darwin.

Subiaco slush… West Coast headquarters was often soft under foot before its 1995 re-development.

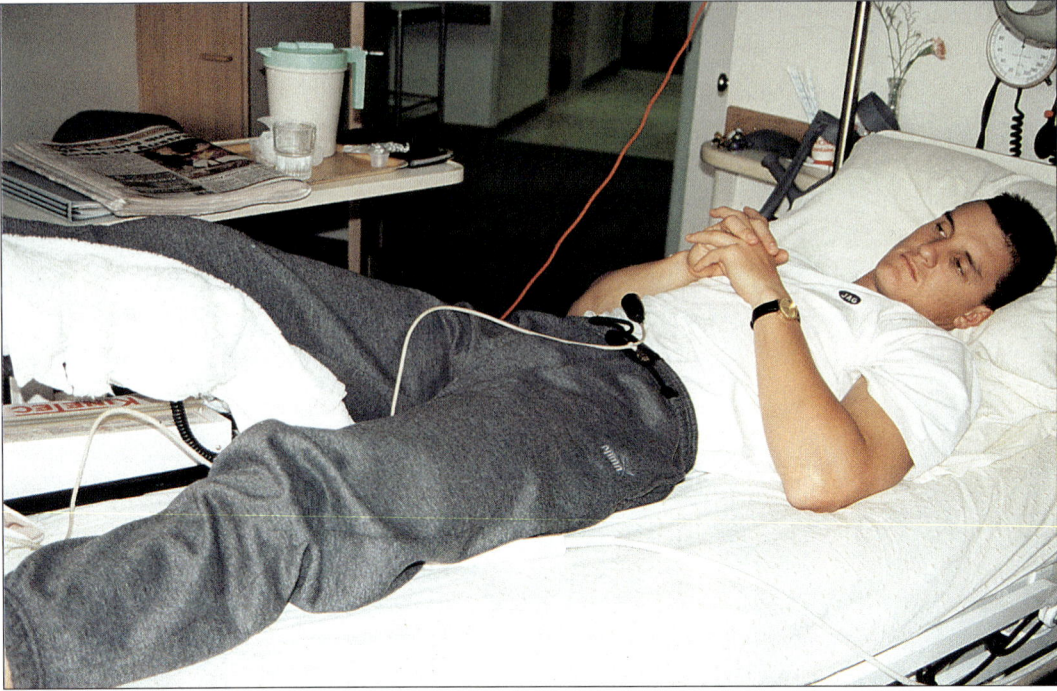
Laid up…Jakovich recuperates in hospital from the knee surgery he required in 1996.

A common sight with Jakovich answering the media's questions.

Golfing glory…One of Jakovich's favourite past times is golf and here he celebrates victory in the West Coast Eagles corporate golf day with his teammates.

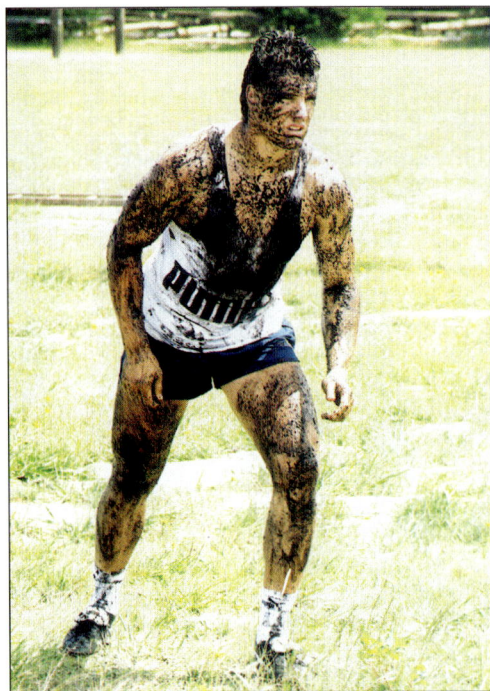

Getting down and dirty… The things we do for a Puma advertising campaign.

Fish feast…Showing off the spoils of another successful dhufish trip.

Always an advocate of a good message Jakovich supports the Quit Campaign.

Another successful trip on the ocean with a beautiful balchin groper.

Jakovich (centre) receives the player of the finals award for 1995.

The King and I…One of the great rivalries of our time, Jakovich and Wayne Carey lock horns and in typical pose jostle for possession.

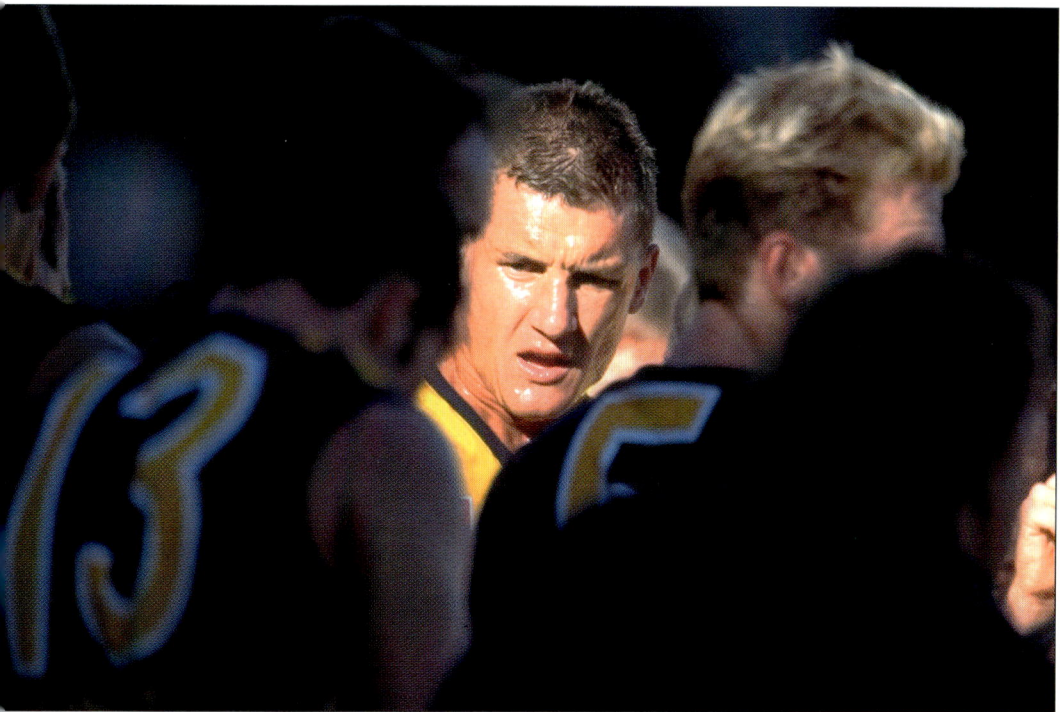

South connection... Scott Watters, Peter Sumich and Jakovich with former Bulldog development officer Mick Moylan who was later a key component of the West Coast recruiting team.

Taking a ride... Sumich and Jakovich soak up the atmosphere at the 1994 grand final parade in Melbourne.

Changing guard...Jakovich shares a moment after celebrating his 250th game with teammate-turned-coach John Worsfold.

Jakovich out muscles St. Kilda's Stephen Powell.

Jakovich is confronted by Collingwood champion Nathan Buckley.

Jakovich bursts clear of Essendon's Ryan O'Connor.

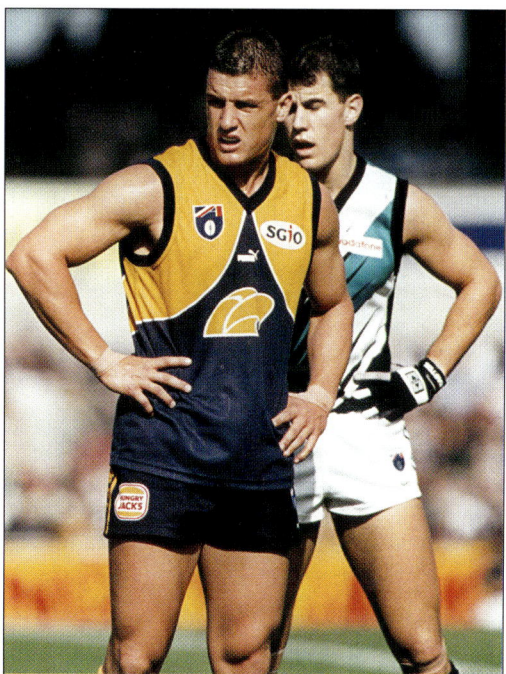

Striking pose... Jakovich and Port Adelaide gladiator Warren Tredrea.

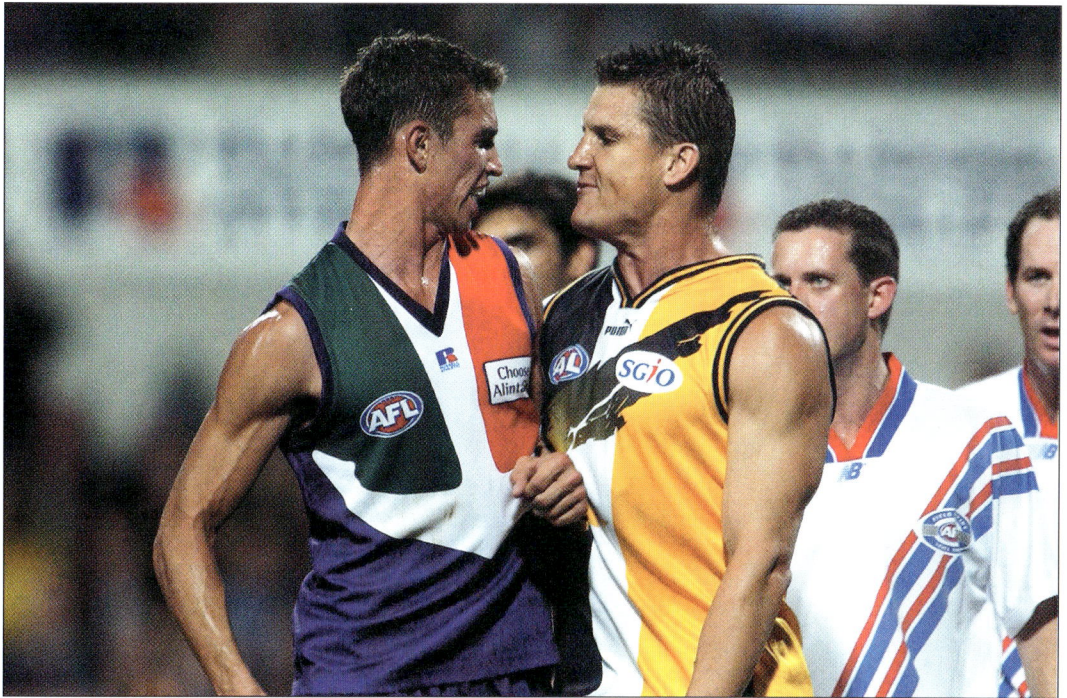

Derby rivalry…There's nothing like a derby to get the competitive juices flowing. Here Jakovich exchanges pleasantries with Fremantle's Troy Simmonds.

Competing with Collingwood young gun Josh Fraser.

Chaired off the ground by teammates after his 201st game (his 200th was played in Sydney). The 201st game was the last at the WACA Ground.

Defensive talent…The six men selected in defence for the West Coast Eagles 10-year all-stars team (back, left to right) Guy McKenna, Jakovich and John Worsfold and (front, left to right) David Hart, Michael Brennan and Ashley McIntosh.

King of the kids…Jakovich has always been keen to encourage the club's young fans.

Jakovich and Carey continued their rivalry even when Carey changed clubs, joining Adelaide in 2003.

Contesting with Melbourne's Russell Robertson.

Family man... Glen with wife Emely while daughters Anique and Jayda are pictured below.

Derby days... Celebrating the team triumph (above) and personal glory (below) as he collects the Ross Glendinning Medal for a best on ground effort.

Sharing a moment with another former teammate-turned-coach, Peter Sumich.

Heading down the race to celebrate another triumph with teammates.

Parting gesture... Jakovich shakes the hand of Melbourne star Jim Stynes as Worsfold moves in.

Daughter Anique in Jakovich's arms before he powered on to Subiaco Oval to celebrate his 250th game in the first match of 2003.

physically. You are short of breath sometimes and it lifts up your arousal levels. You are tense and not very relaxed.

"I knew the procedure I'd had before only took half an hour and I thought I'll just race over to St John of God and get the doctor to do the same procedure, feed the wire up and I will be able to play footy on the weekend. But this time it was a little more complicated. It wasn't the same flutter I had before; it was a fibrillation in the top part of the heart. You have three options; one is to get it back on Amiodarone, which I did. If that doesn't work, you have to go on blood thinning tablets and can't play competitive sport for three months.

"Then there's a procedure where they do an ablation. They put a burn mark on the heart which will get rid of it for ever and a day. But that was something we wanted to steer away from, it's more suitable for 60 or 70-year-olds who might get this condition. That was quite worrying. There is also a drug in America which is fully proven and legal and falls within the Australian drugs code. It's called Ibutalide and is administered through a needle, with a 95 percent rate of rectifying the heart beat within half an hour.

"They were the three options, but the drug isn't available in Australia, so it's expensive and you need a series of permits to bring it into the country. I was on the Amiodarone, hoping that would get it back into rhythm and, if it didn't work, we were going to skip option two and go to option three, which would take three weeks to get here, but would have been for back up.

"Luckily for me, within 72 hours, everything was back to normal. I missed the game against Collingwood when the guys played really well. I was going in every day to get an ECG and on Friday it was still out, Saturday it was still out and they told me to leave it Sunday and just relax. Sometimes when you are on the medication and you mentally take a break it can help. I went back on Monday and everything was okay. I said to Emely when I woke up that I felt okay, I wasn't feeling stressed or up tight.

"They were still going to get Ibutalide in from the US just in case it kicked up on the eve of a final. They could then administer the medication and hope it would kick back in within half an hour. If it happened on a Thursday and we were playing in a preliminary final on the Saturday, that was the thought process behind it – a doctor could administer it and then it would be back into rhythm.

"You can play competitive sport with this condition, you just can't play professional sport with it. You could have a kick around with your mates, you could play indoor soccer or cricket. People live with this for 20 years of their lives, so they can just deal with it. I just had the mentality that the cardiologist said to me that, as easy as the condition came on, it can go away. I got through the footy season and it didn't re-occur.

"But, just after the post-season footy trip, it returned. I had it for three days and it was quite interesting because I had the three options again – the medication, the ablation (which is a better option in the off-season because I wasn't playing competitive sport) and option three, the Ibutalide. We went for option three because we wanted to test it there and then, so, if it flared again during the footy season, we could use it knowing that it would set me right. It was good thinking on the part of the doctors, but unfortunately it didn't work. It didn't work in the half-hour timeframe and I went off to Broome for four days with the family.

"So, Ibutalide was in the system and was going to stay there for 72 hours and hopefully the Amiodarone would work quicker. Exactly what he said happened after we basically mixed the two drugs together. The Ibutalide did work in that sense, but it just didn't kick in as quickly as I had hoped. If it happened on a Friday night before a final, I'd be in a bit of bother. The stuff has a shelf life of only about 12 months anyway. I was in Broome and, on Sunday afternoon, it kicked in. I only started taking the medication on Friday. I now know the condition and how to handle it and I just have to hope it happens on a Monday in the future.

"The whole heart has been thoroughly checked and the cardiologist believes it is as good a heart as he has seen. He also said I have a large heart, although some of my teammates are not convinced of that! People come up to me in the street and ask how I'm doing and they treat me like I have had a triple by-pass, but it's nothing like that."

Going international

THE International Rules series between Australia and Ireland has taken its share of knocks in the last 20 years, but those involved in the heat of battle have embraced the concept. Two years ago, the Irish gave the hybrid game phenomenal support – that passion was transferred to Australian crowds in the 2003 home series. A full house at Subiaco Oval was a great fillip to start the series and, a week later, the Melbourne public also threw its weight behind the second Test at the MCG.

If there were any doubts about the passion generated within the Australian team, they were completely dispelled with a thrilling victory in the Subiaco Oval game. The Australians came from behind to snatch a great win and goalkeeper Glen Jakovich was absolutely ecstatic. In much the same way a Russian soldier marches, legs straight, purposefully up-tempo, Jakovich strode out across the Subiaco Oval turf, arms pumping in triumph. The adrenaline kicked in for a man who had asked the selectors to give him an opportunity in goals and, after being under some early pressure, he responded magnificently to be one of the game's heroes.

"The International Rules series was one of the great experiences, especially after winning," he reflected. "It's their game and we embrace it for a couple of weeks and take on the best in the world at it, so to speak. There is a lot of passion involved. When you pull on a guernsey of any sort, whether it's your club guernsey or State of Origin colours, there is a high level of honour and passion. But when you pull on an Australian jumper and you see the coat of arms, it really hits you.

"I'd never had the opportunity before. In other sports, a cricketer makes his Test debut and is presented with his baggy green cap in an official ceremony in front of the other 11 players. It's a big honour, a great tradition. You see the Wallabies in a Tri-Nation series, in the Bledisloe Cup, against the All Blacks, South Africa, the French or the English and there is a high level of honour, pride and satisfaction. Every four years the Australian soccer team gets the chance to qualify for the World Cup and players just come from everywhere. For us it was more significant because the AFL wanted to play the series in Ireland again last year as they felt there was a big chance of damaging the concept, given that it was going to be up against the Rugby World Cup."

That fear proved to be misplaced – more people attended the Subiaco Oval International Rules match than Perth's blockbuster World Cup rugby clash between England and South Africa. When Ireland arrived on Australian shores they again talked up the disadvantages they faced because they were amateurs. Clearly, that irked the Australian players.

"The Irish said their players, being amateurs, really looked forward to touring Australia to represent their country," says Jakovich. "So the AFL decided to take the rugby head-on and, because Perth had not staged an International Rules match for 10 years, they decided to play one of the games here. It sold out in 10 days, with 41,000 people at Subiaco Oval, which was just unbelievable.

"The game was so quick – I had a lot of friends who said the action was so constant they didn't have time to go to the toilet – it was just full-on for 80 minutes. I trained and played for WA against the Irish and knew it was going to be quick and I needed to work on my angles, my lines and obviously get my defenders looking after me so there weren't too many holes for the Irishmen to slide into and score.

"When Ireland scored a goal early in the first Test match, there wasn't a lot I could do about it. I didn't get down on myself because they had a 4-2 situation and were on a fast break. When I look back on the video, I probably should have come off my line a bit quicker. I got a piece on it, which was what was so disappointing. From then I thought 'well, there wasn't a lot I could do about that, so I just need to get on with it.' My goal was to go in at quarter-time with a clean sheet and at the end of the night I had three good quarters.

"I felt some pressure early because the match committee were worried about going with me. What got me over the line was exactly what Australian coach Garry Lyon said at the camp in Bunbury; 'what you put into this is what you will get out of it.' I knew I had put a lot into it before going to the camp. I was training with Stewie Cormack, the West Coast fitness coach, who also filled that role for the Australian team, and I trained with good friend Jason Petkovic, the Perth Glory goalkeeper, and also worked with his goalkeeping coach Willie McNally, who had played Gaelic football.

"I learnt a lot before I got to the camp and, once there, I started a bit slow in goals, but got better with every day. They could see that, but they were still worried whether I would be up to it. I knew I would be all right and that's where you have to stay strong within yourself. They're wondering before the game and I'm thinking, I don't need this pressure, because I don't have to prove anything to anyone. But then I realised, that wasn't the attitude to have because I put that pressure on myself. I put my hand up and asked for the role, so I couldn't back out of the agreement. So I thought I'm just going to get out there and have one helluva crack."

While Jakovich had faced some big opponents in his long and illustrious career, he came away from that International Rules match absolutely spent. He probably covered less ground than in any other game in his career, but he was fatigued.

"I was probably the most exhausted mentally after that game than ever before," he said. "I nearly fainted after the game. How could I be exhausted as a goalkeeper? It was the only time in my 14 years that I'd come off without a bruise, without a bump, but I felt so much pressure after the game. The doctor came over and said I looked like a ghost, he took my blood pressure... all that was because of the mental application I put in.

"For the whole 80 minutes I had to concentrate. It's not like you can relax when the ball is cleared out of your zone because the game is so quick. Basically I was being a dictator to my back men (Leo Barry, Luke Power, Matthew Scarlett, Jarred Crouch and Chris Johnson) to get them to cover the holes and then get support from blokes like Rohan Smith and Brad Johnson, who ran back. From that aspect it was good, but it was a very, very stressful 80 minutes.

"When I look at the video, I think I over-did the celebrations a bit. But I'm not ashamed of it. When you put a lot into something and you are desperate to play for your country and when you win in a series or a game which favours the opposition, then you do get really excited. What people tend to forget is that you had 41,000 fans going ballistic. I hadn't heard Subiaco Oval like that since we beat Hawthorn in the elimination final of 1992 by 13 points. They were that loud, parochial and fanatical... they were phenomenal. It was just a great experience; a great relief, but it was also a great sense of accomplishment.

"Losing the second match didn't worry me either. That loss didn't take any gloss off the series win because that was what we were after... we lost the second game at the MCG by only three points anyway. We got off to a real slow start again and they got away to a flier. They got two past me early, one was a bad move by myself and the other one there was nothing I could do about it because he turned the defender inside out and I had no chance.

"It's a game where, as the goalkeeper, you have to stay on your line for the most part but, in some circumstances, you have to come off it. Sometimes it's too late and that's no fault of yours, it's the way the ball has come in. From that aspect I let two in during the first quarter, but had a clean sheet after that. Dipper (Robert DiPierdomenico) said to me after the second game that I should be well-pleased with what I'd done because I had let three goals in during the series and my Irish counterpart let in four and he's a full-time goalie.

"The reception we had in Melbourne was unbelievable. There were 60,000 people and it out-did the rugby union the next night between Australia and Ireland which had 54,000 at Telstra Stadium."

Before the Melbourne game, the players were also buoyed by the news that support for the series guaranteed its future. New AFL CEO Andrew Demetriou addressed the players, congratulated them on their commitment and said that, because of their contribution, the future of the series had been shored up.

"Andrew Demetriou spoke to the players before the game and said we were fantastic ambassadors for our sport and an agreement had been signed for another nine years, so it will go through until 2012," Jakovich said. "They were so rapt with this team, they reckoned it was the best Australia had ever put together.

"They are looking at sending two teams to Ireland next time and playing some sort of a round robin series, where we can really promote it. To be part of something which was so successful on and off the ground was very gratifying. It was fantastic to play with guys who have achieved so much in their football – I got a lot out of spending two weeks with different teammates and we became united. It was like I had played with Brad Johnson or Luke Power or Matthew Pavlich for five years. We got on so well."

While Demetriou might have been delighted with the commitment of the players, the Aussies upset a few VIPs as they kept the official after-series party waiting because they were enjoying an impromptu moment of their own in the MCG dressing room.

"When we came off the MCG, after the presentation and singing the national anthem, there was a function scheduled upstairs, but we turned up about an hour late," Jakovich said. "We were still down in the rooms getting photos with the cup. It started with the North Melbourne guys, jokingly saying how about we have our photo taken with the cup. So someone started singing the Kangaroos theme song and we all joined in. Then we went through the whole 16 AFL clubs, even the ones that weren't represented by players. Port Adelaide didn't have a player, but the doctor was from there.

"I'll never forget that moment which symbolised how 16 clubs had come together to represent their country. To be part of that was so fulfilling – it ranks in the top five experiences of my career, after the premierships and some great finals results. The Irish had come out to Australia and said they were worried about the physical presence of the Australians because we are professional athletes... Garry Lyon said 'well, let's not disappoint them.'"

If the Irish were expecting the series to be physical, then the Australians delivered, although a couple of incidents in the Perth Test were probably a little inflated – they resulted in Adelaide star Mark Bickley and Geelong's All-Australian defender Matthew Scarlett going to the tribunal and being subsequently suspended for the second Test.

"The Bickley incident didn't need to go to the tribunal," says Jakovich. "It was dealt with at the time with a yellow card and he was off for 15 minutes. I didn't see the Scarlett incident, but obviously it happened and he was disappointed with that.

"The Irish had no ill-feelings about it; everyone has to abide by the game's rules and, as far as they were concerned, they gave it their best shot and the Australians were just too good. The Irish did a bit of niggling, they had a go and we gave it back to them. They put a few of the Australian players on their backsides too. It was a bit odd that they would take a physical approach to the game when they were 21-points up half-way through the first quarter in Perth.

"In both games we knew our fitness would get them in the second half. They were trying to make it a one-on-one contest, where their skills with the round ball would give them the edge. They wanted to play the game on their terms, kick to the open spaces where their pace could present problems for us, but we wanted to keep it a tight contest, bottle it up, get the ball on the ground and get them looking. So it was two different game plans going head-to-head and ours prevailed."

The years ahead

JAKOVICH believes that, because he set such high standards throughout his career, he became a media target – but the return of his close friend as coach rejuvenated his career.

"The last five weeks of 2001 were tough," he said reflectively. "Very stressful... you just have to call upon every ounce of courage in your body to say 'well, I'm not going to lay down and let them walk all over me.' The fight wasn't as resilient as it could have been, but I knew that playing on one leg and without a fitness base, I still got by, I still played 22 games. I didn't have as shocking a season as some media people thought. It wasn't good, but it wasn't that bad either. It was probably because I set such high standards in the first 10 years of my career. When I look back on 13 years, there were a couple of vintage seasons when we won premierships, but I would rate the first year under John in the best four or five.

"We came back against all odds to turn the club's fortunes around in such a short period, with membership and sponsors growing again; the playing group grew stronger; and then we backed it up again. We have muscled our way in there to have a serious crack at it in the next three or four years."

Jakovich believes it takes time to achieve the levels of belief and consistency required to compete successfully at AFL, but that the young West Coast Eagles squad has taken giant strides towards making a serious tilt at a third premiership.

"You can never replace a John Worsfold or a Guy McKenna with another John Worsfold or Guy McKenna, but you can replace them with an Adam Selwood or a Darren Glass, who have proved they can compete at the level... they just need to do it on a consistent basis," he says. "Playing in big games and performing consistently are the two main criteria. And, once you do that, you become a bona-fide footballer. We have one of the youngest groups in the competition and we're two or three years away, but we are now playing finals football and our guys have to be mentally prepared and mentally strong for that reason.

"Because we've had Ashley and myself back in defence for so long, people have taken it for granted. It will take a bit of time, but there are players who can do the job and who will become good footballers in those positions. It's a matter of growing into the role, maturing into the role and playing regular, consistent football. In a season you need to string together eight to 10 good games where you are consistent and on top of your game.

"What happens then is that the opposition knows they are coming up against a defender who is in good touch, good form, hard at it, very disciplined and that gets the key forward thinking about his game and about how he's going to get into it and have an impact. Once that mechanism is in place, it's time for players stand up and say 'I want that position.' Just as I said when I was 18. It comes down to the individual and the match committee, who put so much work into the development of the younger guys; we will get it right and we will replace the experienced players.

"John realises the honeymoon period is over. Now it's a matter of moving forward and that could mean that, in the next year or two, we have to take a step back to go forward. Whether that means we have to trade a name player, who is not in the right mix for us, that's up to the match committee and the club. The challenge for the match committee is to get a squad which is going to play together for the next six years. That is where you make decisions with McDougall and Lynch, for example. Obviously I won't be there, so John and the match committee need about 28 guys who can have a serious crack at it, along similar lines to Brisbane. They had 16 guys who were triple premiership players. After that, they have top-up players who do a job when required. We're a good half-dozen players away from that. We have four or five in our squad, but they have to mature and come on now. That's where we are at.

"John needs to virtually wipe the slate clean of guys he played a lot of footy with. He played a little with Ben Cousins, Michael Gardiner, Michael Braun, Chad Morrison, but there are only two premiership players left – myself and Drew Banfield, so I don't think it's a big issue. Dean Laidley has about 10 premiership teammates he's got to coach at the Kangaroos, so that's an issue and obviously a lot harder."

Establishing the right time to retire has also involved plenty of consideration for Jakovich. And he knows a fairytale climax is unlikely.

"People say here's a chance to go out on a good note – that's what they said at the end of the 2003 season, because my last couple of games were high quality," Jakovich said. But the only good note to go out on is to kick the winning goal in a grand final, to play in a premiership, to play in a winning Derby in your last game... but they're fairy tales. They happen once in a blue moon.

"My ideal way to go is to bow out after I've done everything I can; that I have given it everything and I just can't do any more. The worst thing an athlete can do, not a footballer, but simply any kind of athlete, is to go into retirement too early. The body and the mind play funny games and, if I had retired last year, you could bet your bottom dollar that by April, May or June after six months off, I would start to feel good in the body and I'd be watching some 30-year-olds running around and thinking 'that crab's still there, maybe I gave the game away too early.' By that stage it's too late and I would have to go to my grave always wondering whether I gave the game up too early. So ,for me, apart from playing in a winning grand final, the best way to finish this journey I started as a seven-year-old kid is to call it quits when I can't go any more.

"After my retirement at the end of this season, I want to go into the workforce. I enjoy working and grew up in an environment dominated by blue collar workers. I haven't thought about coaching, I've got a few business interests I'd like to remain involved with, and I'll probably stay involved with the football club in some capacity."

The football world at large has this image of Glen Jakovich etched deeply into its psyche. He's big, strong, bold, imposing and passionate; a Robocop figure with bulging biceps and a drive to succeed. At home, though, it's a different story. The 31-year-old father of two performs the daily parenting tasks as a matter of course. He changes dirty nappies and completes other duties expected of a father in this era. With wife Emely, whom he met at primary school, he dotes on his young daughters Anique (3) and Jayda, who is just a few months old.

"He is very much a hands-on dad," said Emely, who has seen Glen blossom from teenage prodigy to one of the most successful players in AFL history. "The second, we were hoping for a boy, only because of the pigeon pair thing, but we wouldn't change it for the world now. Jayda is just gorgeous."

Emely and Glen met at school and also knew each other through a family connection, both families often frequenting the Spearwood Dalmatinac Soccer Club. It wasn't until Emely had finished school that romance blossomed, but she had already taken a keen interest in Glen's football.

"I was a good friend of Glen's first cousin," she said. "And I used to go to the football at South Fremantle quite often with Deanne. Because of her link to Glen, we took an interest in how he played and I am a bit surprised to see how his career has been shaped. I started going out with Glen in 1990, then we broke up for a little while, so I wasn't at the 1991 grand final. I was there in 1992, though and we have been together ever since.

"It will be quite scary to think what will happen with football now coming to an end because it has been such a big part of our lives. Every second week for more than a decade I've got used to Glen going to an away game, so there will be some big adjustments to make. Glen tends not to bring his football problems home with him – if he is in a form slump, or is down on himself for whatever reason, it doesn't really affect his home life. There is no time, with the kids needing attention, for him to dwell too much on his football concerns."

Emely Jakovich

Tributes

It is true to say that Mick Malthouse had some initial reservations about the highly talented Jakovich, yet there is a sense of pride in his voice as he espouses the virtues of the four-times West Coast Eagles Club Champion.

"Glen has been an enthusiastic team member throughout his career and has always thrived on the contest," says Malthouse. "He has given respect to people in authority – if all players were like him you would always come through.

"He had an outstanding record against Wayne Carey, the player I consider to be the best I've ever seen, and there are a couple of games I can remember specifically relating to Glen. There was a game against Melbourne, a final. The week before, David Schwartz had kicked eight goals against Footscray and Garry Lyon had kicked a bag a week before that, so we were going into the game against a potent Melbourne attack. Glen, who was always a very good mark, was going to play on Schwartz and he came to me and said 'I'm going to play on him and I'm just going to punch the ball every opportunity I get in the first half until I destroy the confidence he will take into the game.' He did that job brilliantly, became a very good attacking weapon for us in the second half and, at one stage, I thought he was going to kick the goal of the year. He ran about two-thirds the length of the ground and had a long shot at goal which hit the post.

"There was another game, I remember, which was in stark contrast. Glen set himself to play on Carey in this particular game at the MCG and thought that if he couldn't beat Carey then we wouldn't win the game. As it turned out, he got absolutely belted by Carey, but we won the game. It was a great lesson for Glen because it showed him that we weren't a one-man band. In another game against Carey at Waverley, I recall Glen holding Carey to only two or three possessions while getting more than 20 himself. His record against Wayne was outstanding, he probably had a 75-80% winning record against Carey and that speaks volumes for the quality player that Glen has been.

"There was always a good chemistry between Glen and myself. We always got on very well. He never argued with me, he always accepted responsibility if I thought he had played poorly. There was a terrific mutual respect. At three-quarter time in the last game I coached for the Eagles against Carlton, I wished him well and he had a tear in his eye. So did I."

Mick Malthouse

"When Glen Jakovich arrived at the West Coast Eagles, he was obviously a very young man, but initially we had trouble understanding him, particularly on-field. A measure of his youth was that he had mouth guards, both top and bottom, because he had braces on his teeth. When we played Melbourne at the MCG one year I spent the week leading up to it asking Jak to teach me how to say 'I'm going to kill ya' in Croatian.' I practised it and tried to get the accent and the inflection right. I practised and practised and practised and then ran down to Jako's brother Allan at the start of the game and threw all these Croatian words at him. I don't know if he thought it was a proper death threat or if he saw the humorous side of it. Because I said it in Croatian, I think he was half in shock.

"Even if Glen was dominating with best-on-ground performances and winning the footy, I would remind him every 10 minutes to man up. If he ran down the ground and kicked a goal or kicked it to Suma at full-forward, I would be screaming at him to get back on his man. I'd be telling him to not jog back to the applause of the crowd, but to get back on his man and focus on the next contest. I was pretty hard on him, he could have been dominating and beating his man, but I always brought him back to the disciplines that we were on about as a side.

"It's pretty tough to single out the best players ever to play for the club. Going on a lot of different criteria – going on club champion awards, Jako and Cousins are right up there. On what Glen's achieved with club champion awards through a great era, it's outstanding. Going on value to the side over a long period of time, you have Mainwaring, McKenna, Kemp, McIntosh.

"When Glen hurt his knee, of all the guys I've seen requiring knee reconstructions, the impact it had on him, as a person, was greater than any others. The other guys had certain mechanisms to cope, whereas it was unbelievable how much it affected him. It took weeks for him to get over it mentally before he started his physical recovery. Whether he thought his career was over or that he was going to miss more than two or three games in a row, he just didn't know how to cope with 'I can't play football.' I had a good chat to him. I tried to talk about what I did when I hurt my knee, told him to set some new goals that weren't around playing, and do a better knee rehabilitation than anyone has ever done and set a new standard in that, like he did with his training. Rather than just think 'I'll cruise through this and I'll be a great player again', I told him he had an opportunity to do something different and set some standards in that. We spent a lot of time just walking together, walking laps, jogging, sitting on bikes alongside each other. I just let him know that we were going to both be ready for the start of the next season."

John Worsfold

Almost a decade and a half later, one of the most decorated junior careers in WA history has been emulated at senior level; Jakovich won the club champion award four times, was an All-Australian in 1994 and 1995 and a premiership player in 1992 and 1994. Having achieved so highly in an outstanding team, Jakovich will naturally always be mentioned in debates over who is the best player to represent the club. Of course, such an argument is always subjective, but Nisbett agrees that Jakovich will always figure highly in those discussions.

"It is always a difficult argument as to the best player ever to play for the club," Nisbett said. "Certainly Glen has had as much influence on the game as any player. At his very best, Glen would just dominate a game, he would destroy the opposition and turn defence into attack all the time.

"I couldn't really rate one player the best ever, but certainly he's in the very, very top echelon – he's one of the best because, forget his best and fairests, it's about his quality of play, his consistency... he played almost every week. He is just a wonderful footballer and did everything to get the best out of himself. His preparation is outstanding. I can't think of a year when Glen reported for training at the start of pre-season out of condition.

"He might have had problems with injury where he couldn't train because of surgery and the many operations he's had, but he would always be in pristine condition and a true professional in every sense. He was no different to other players who let their hair down a bit straight after the season, but he had a schedule he kept to and knew when he had to start getting back into training and that's why he's been such a wonderful player.

"Glen had to wait a bit longer for his initial opportunity than he wanted. Ashley McIntosh played before him, but again it was a question of keeping Glen's expectations under wraps – Mick was very much aware of that and delaying his entry into AFL football was probably a good thing for Glen. If he had got into the team easily, it might have affected his performances over those first couple of years. He was ready to play at the start of the season, but the match committee thought that by leaving it a bit longer would help him - and it did.

"He played eight or nine games with South Fremantle and was runner-up in their fairest and best, so he was in good form, ready to play and every week he was a big topic of conversation at match committee meetings. The biggest thing was trying to explain to him that he had some deficiencies. Often, with a highly talented young player coming through – and Glen was dominant – junior coaches are reluctant to point out the deficiencies in a 17 or 18-year-old, so they think they have done it all.

"It was a really difficult thing for a young player to understand. We believed that he also had received some pretty poor advice from some people who said 'you are a budding champion and you're going to do this and you're going to do that.' But the work has to come before the champion status can be confirmed. Certainly Glen did a lot of work to get to where he is."

Jakovich was the cornerstone of a wonderful defence during the club's dominant years and, although the club is still relatively young, it's doubtful whether there will ever be a half-back line to rival that of Guy McKenna, Jakovich and John Worsfold.

"I don't think any club – maybe with the exceptions of the great Richmond and Carlton teams – had half-back lines like that," says Nisbett. "I can't think of anything to compare with that half-back line, particularly if you include (Chris) Waterman and (Dean) Laidley, who were terrific players. Chris could play anywhere, but often found himself at half-back. Dean missed four games a year with us because of sheer weight of numbers and would have played with any other team in the competition. It was just an outstanding half-back line.

"It was a dominant and very, very good backline. The side was built around a mentality of strangling the opposition and then piling on the offensive pressure. The West Coast Eagles weren't renowned for their defensive skills when Mick got here and, consequently, that turned them around.

"Mind you, Glen wasn't always the tightest checking defender going around, but the balance between McKenna, Jakovich, Worsfold, (Ashley) McIntosh, (Michael) Brennan, (David) Hart, Laidley and Waterman certainly made life a little easier for Glen to do his job as well as he did. The side might have been built around defence, but the centreline players had a fair bit to do with the success as well. It was a great midfield."

In this age of salary cap pressures and close AFL scrutiny, the management of any club's total player payments scheme is crucial. And, often, those payments cannot be harnessed without the support of senior players.

Glen Jakovich is one man who has always been willing to re-negotiate his contract in the interests of offering the club flexibility in maintaining the best possible playing list. Trevor Nisbett has been closely involved with many of those contract negotiations.

"Glen has always been accommodating with the football club and has been happy to vary his contract to fit another player on the list," Nisbett said. "He has been happy to extend his contract to do the same. I don't think there has ever been a time when Glen has said 'look, no I can't.' From a professional point of view, he always understood the football club's position when we were trying to get the best squad together. No other club has ever spoken to him because he's one of those guys other clubs would probably consider a franchise player and one the club would never let go.

"He will be judged as one of the best centre half-backs ever to pull on a boot, but he also has been a terrific club man. Glen has grown as a person in his time at the club. When he first came here, his thoughts were footy, footy, footy. He had the attitude that he was going to get as much out of this as he could. It didn't take him long to realise he was going to need other people.

"Your priority when you are a footballer is yourself. But he has grown as a person to the point where he understands the club structure, he understands the AFL, he has worked with the Players' Association, so he understands the needs of other players. He has also worked very hard with a young leadership group here to assist them after the disappointment of not being captain of the club.

"He has been a vice-captain, he has been in all those roles, and I guess, as a person, he has grown enormously over the 14 years. Glen's from humble beginnings, but he has made something of his life and his career and he understands how tough it is out there for a lot of young people. Some of the things he has done with charity work, with working for the footy club, dealing with the sponsors and assisting with community projects, has seen him learn more about himself and that is why he has grown into such a quality person.

"He is an outstanding ambassador. He has been very loyal to the club, his family and sponsors. He has grown in stature with every year. Hopefully, he will continue to work with the club for years to come when his career comes to an end."

Trevor Nisbett

Sometimes, because the West Coast Eagles play the majority of their games away from the Melbourne football hub, players from the Perth-based club are not afforded their due recognition. But former Carlton captain and football great Stephen Kernahan, who received an early insight into Jakovich's capabilities, believes the West Coast man-mountain received the respect he deserved.

"Certainly Glen Jakovich was held in the highest possible regard from his peers," said Kernahan, whose 226 games as skipper of the Blues is an AFL record. "I don't think he missed out in any way in terms of the respect he earned because he was playing most of his football over there."

While Jakovich had to wait until mid-season in 1991 for his first opportunity, once he was afforded that chance he was thrown in at the deep end, to such an extent that in his third game he stood Kernahan, one of the all-time greats at Carlton. As a measure of Kernahan's credentials, consider these facts. He was named at centre half-forward in Carlton's team of the century, he played 251 games, was a three-time Carlton fairest and best, kicked a club record 738 goals and was 11 times the Blues leading goal-kicker. They don't come much greater than the South Australian champion, who started his career with Glenelg.

"I don't remember specifics about the first time I played on Glen, but I do remember coming up against him in the early stages of his career," Kernahan said. "I didn't realise it was his third game, but my first impression was that he was a pretty big boy. After that first clash, when he did pretty well, he just got better and better. Along with Hawthorn's Chris Langford, I found him one of the toughest opponents I ever came up against and I never had too many good games against him. Later in my career when I was used more at full-forward, he would sometimes come back to the goal square with me but, just as often, I was picked up by someone like Ashley McIntosh. It was never easy playing against West Coast.

"Jako started at the Eagles at a time when they were in their power surge and they had a great back line. Players like John Worsfold were already established and they were outstanding in the back half. There weren't a lot of teams that had a good record against them and no-one enjoyed playing against them, particularly in Perth. I just remember Glen as being big and strong. I wasn't blessed with a lot of pace and he could certainly go with me and he was always very good at spoiling. As a forward, the first couple of contests would set the standard for the day and, if a high ball came in early on, he would really belt it away. You would then be thinking that the ball would need to come in good if you were going to have a good day.

"Glen has obviously had a great career; the team used to frustrate me a bit because we would use a zone defence on the kick-ins and he would often be the Eagles second target, running down the wing. He's being used as a forward a lot these days. I wish they did that with him a bit when I was playing!"

Stephen Kernahan

"This [sense of loyalty] was the attitude he carried to West Coast. Sure, he was the best centre half-back in the 1990s, but it was giving to the team and loyalty to the team that he expressed best. Many great players are selfish, thinking only of personal glory, but Glen has. and always will, put the team ahead of personal glory. These attributes were instilled into him by his Dad in early childhood and he carried them through to high school and then to West Coast.

"*Sedulus et audax* is the Latin motto on the family crest; it means zealous and bold, or diligent and daring – both interpretations are characteristic of Glen. Without doubt, he is zealous about his football and his ambition to be a top-flight footballer was a childhood dream that he converted to reality. Glen is a zealot in the way he was prepared to sacrifice a lot during his teenage years to get to where he is today. Team glory and then personal best was always his way; poor performance and, at times, under achievement, was met by a steely resolve to rectify the situation.

"In the face of adversity, whether that be the loss of his father, a knee reconstruction or shoulder problems, he never lost sight of his goal of being the best he could for both the team and himself. I think this is also exemplified over the Eagles captaincy. A lesser person might have been devastated at missing the captaincy of West Coast a couple of years ago and allowed it to affect them for the duration of their career. Naturally, he was very disappointed, but instead of wallowing in self-pity, he got behind Ben Cousins and the team. Only zealots who put the cause ahead of personal glory are capable of that accomplishment.

"His boldness is exemplified by his style of play – a free-wheeling centre half-back who was prepared to back himself, leave his opponent and gain possession and then bounce his way into attack. It was simply breathtaking. The crowd loved it, even more so when it happened against Wayne Carey. This boldness allowed coach Mick Malthouse to build his dynasty around a 'Rock of Gibraltar', but really Glen was an omnipresent Zeus-like figure who patrolled the back half and boldly led counter attack after counter attack.

"After Glen's knee reconstruction, he had many doubts as to whether he would return to his glory days and some indifferent form placed added pressure on him. One day he said to me, 'Grano, if I can win one more fairest and best then I'll know I've got back to what I was.' I told him that he could do it if he approached that goal single-mindedly. On the night of the club champion award in 2000, I received a call at about 11.15pm from Glen to tell me he had won the fairest and best. It was a great moment and I believe it re-launched his career, although Glen and the club had a terrible 2001 season.

"Glen always wanted to prove his knockers wrong – from his high school days and right through to this day. Often the criticism he received was overdone.

"Glen never forgot his roots or the people who helped him get to where he got. His loyalty to family is obvious. Often, when we are out, people would come up and say hello to Glen. He would introduce me as his former teacher and people would give him a funny look, like what are you doing talking to your old teacher? He would then tell them about the old days and, in the process, acknowledge me. It always was appreciated. He would run into old school mates he hadn't seen in years and would go out of his way to say hello.

"Glen never lost his identity and values and never got caught up in the fame game. That's why he is loved by the football public."

Tony Granich

Champion North Melbourne and Adelaide centre half-forward Wayne Carey, regarded by many as the greatest player of his time, ranks Glen Jakovich as the best player he ever found himself pitted against.

High praise indeed from the lynchpin of twin North Melbourne premierships and a man who often found himself opposed to Carlton's full-back of the century Stephen Silvagni. While Silvagni was listed at full-back in the team of the century in 1996, Carey rates Jakovich as his superior, not just because of his defensive qualities, but also because of his capacity to win possession.

"He has been a fantastic player and I would rate him slightly ahead of Carlton's Stephen Silvagni as the best I have played against," Carey assessed. "Not only was Glen exceptional in the man-on-man battle at stopping his opponent, but he won a lot of the ball himself. We all play footy to get the ball and he was able to do that. He was very skilful and often racked up 20 or 30 possessions. He played in a defence that boasted some outstanding players and combined with blokes like Guy McKenna, John Worsfold and others made it tough to beat them.

"I never really kept score on the record between the two of us and there were occasions when one of us was crook as well. I remember at Subiaco Oval when Glen had an ankle injury and obviously wasn't feeling the best and I had a pretty good day. When it's all over we will probably sit down and have a beer together. Actually we did last year when we were at a sportsman's night together. I'm sure I will run into Glen in the future at another charity function.

"The result of our clash didn't always reflect the result of the game. I remember a final in 1997 when I didn't play well, but the team won and there were other occasions when I went reasonably well, but the team lost."

The rivalry between Carey and Jakovich started early in their careers and blossomed to the point where it was one of the great match-ups of their era. The contest-within-a-contest was usually absorbing, sometimes more so than the game itself, and both men have great respect for each other.

"The first time I played on Glen, I thought he was a pretty big lad," said Carey. "He is a little younger than me, but I was thinking 'gee, he's a big boy.' From memory I did all right in that first game. You always go out to play well, but every time you're matched up against an opponent where you have built a bit of a rivalry, you try to find that bit extra. I reckon Jako is probably up by a couple in our head-to-head battle. I never really kept score, I suppose that's what the media threw at us, but we were two very competitive people and I think we both enjoyed the contests.

"The game has changed in the last few years and it's rare for players to now settle in one position and stay there. Even during our battles, I would often take Glen to full-back where we felt he was probably less comfortable. It has been like that for a few years now, with player versatility meaning guys are thrown into different roles from quarter to quarter, let alone game to game, although the Buckley-Voss head-to-head battle seems to have survived. But I don't think we will see rivalries like the Stephen Silvagni-Tony Lockett clashes that were always such a highlight.

"It's a pity this will be the last year Glen and I will play against each other, because this will be my last season as well. I hope there is the chance for one last battle because, as I said, we both enjoy the contest."

Wayne Carey

Best of the Eagles

ONE OF the first things fans will notice about the Glen Jakovich West Coast Eagles all-stars team is that he has selected himself at centre half-back. That selection was made after some pressure from the author and because a West Coast team without Jakovich at centre half-back could not be considered a genuine all-stars team. So here is Jakovich's appraisal of his celebrated teammates, most of whom played in premiership teams with him in 1992 or 1994.

David Hart

"A terrific player who was part of the inaugural West Coast team. He missed the 1992 grand final when he strained a hamstring in the WAFL preliminary final, but was back for 1994. A cheeky back pocket player who thrived on attention."

Ashley McIntosh

"Ranks with Chris Langford and Stephen Silvagni as the best full-back I played with or against, with very little separating the three of them. I often wondered how good he could have been had his body been in better nick."

Michael Brennan

"A hard-nosed competitor who was part of the club's inaugural squad; having a player of his ability to learn from was a great benefit to all us younger guys. He could tackle players of varying sizes and strengths."

Guy McKenna

"One of the most gifted players I have seen who complemented the rest of the defensive group. He wasn't always as accountable as other guys, but his ability to run off and create was one of his strengths. Used the ball very well."

John Worsfold

"What can I say? A fabulous leader, but often under-rated as a player. He won a club champion award as a midfielder before making the switch to defence and it was a privilege to play alongside him. He did all the team things brilliantly."

Peter Matera

"One of the most exciting and devastating players I've ever seen. His performance in the 1992 grand final, kicking five goals off a wing, must rank as one of the all-time great efforts."

West Coast all-stars

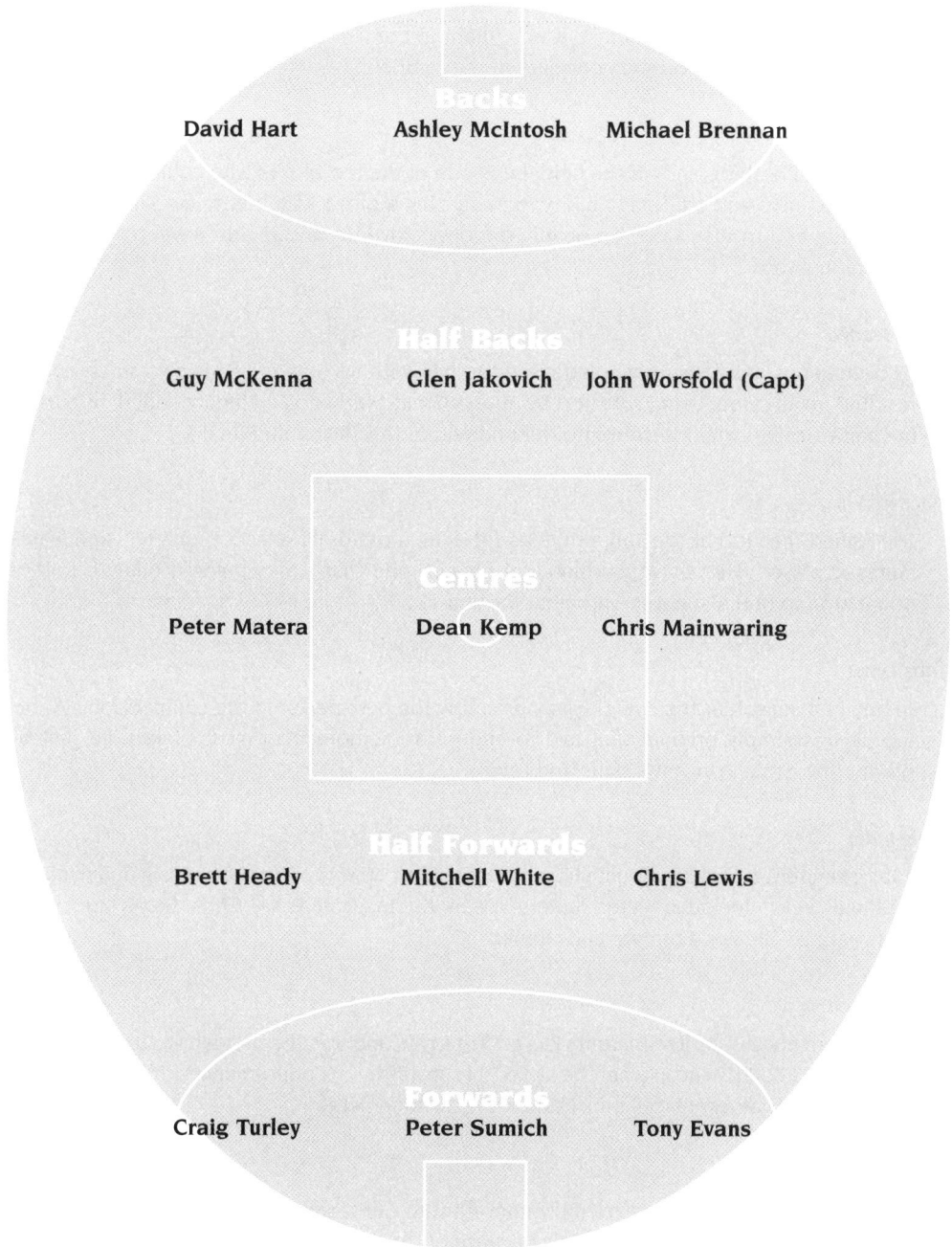

Backs

David Hart   Ashley McIntosh   Michael Brennan

Half Backs

Guy McKenna   Glen Jakovich   John Worsfold (Capt)

Centres

Peter Matera   Dean Kemp   Chris Mainwaring

Half Forwards

Brett Heady   Mitchell White   Chris Lewis

Forwards

Craig Turley   Peter Sumich   Tony Evans

Ruck:	**Michael Gardiner**	**Ben Cousins**	**Don Pyke**
Interchange:	**Chris Waterman**	**Drew Banfield**	**Chris Judd**	**Phil Matera**
Emergencies:	**Dwayne Lamb**	**Peter Wilson**	**Ryan Turnbull**

Dean Kemp

"Silky smooth skills and one of the most gifted players of our time. He rates among the best players I've played with or against; was brilliant in the clinches and was able to hit targets, despite being under enormous pressure in the midfield."

Chris Mainwaring

"Played hard both on and off the field; he is one of the few blokes who could enjoy a lively social existence and still play quality football. It's a pity a knee injury virtually brought a premature end to his career... probably the best player from our club never to win a club champion award."

Brett Heady

"A courageous half-forward who attacked the ball with no regard for his own safety, which resulted in his career being cut short by injury. Great overhead and highly skilled, he turned the game around when thrown into the midfield in the 1992 grand final."

Mitchell White

"He joined the club at the same time as I did, as a pre-draft selection in 1990, and was a fantastic player. He was very athletic for his size and that agility made it difficult for the opposition to find a suitable opponent for him."

Chris Lewis

"In my first season at the club, he was probably the best player in the competition. At his top he was simply brilliant and had to endure a lot more than most blokes did just by playing the game. Uncanny skills and tough."

Craig Turley

"Unfortunately, a back injury cut short his career, but he was an important cog in a dynamic midfield which included Peter Matera, Dean Kemp, Don Pyke, Chris Lewis and Chris Mainwaring. He was a prolific ball-winner."

Peter Sumich

"His record speaks for itself. Suma kicked 514 goals and was the first left-footer to kick 100 goals in a VFL/AFL season when he kicked 111 in 1991. His performances in finals, with 62 goals from 19 games, places him 12th on the all-time list."

Tony Evans

"A tough little nut who was extremely important to our team. A typical in-and-under rover who was restricted to 109 games only because of the selfless way he played. He kicked two crucial goals for us just before half-time in the 1992 grand final."

Michael Gardiner

"Has emerged in the past couple of years as the best ruckman in our club's history and will only get better. This year was also elevated to a vice-captaincy role and he has the ability to become one of the club's great players."

Ben Cousins

"Has already won three club champion awards and, at 25, should still have his best years ahead of him. He and Gardiner will be important players as the club pushes to recreate history."

Don Pyke

"Turned his career around after some problems initially, converting his free-running goal-kicking game into the close-checking midfielder that Mick Malthouse wanted. Showed great courage to come back in the 1992 grand final after being knocked out by Gary Ablett."

Chris Waterman

"Our Mr Fixit for so long. Able to play forward, back or midfield, Muddy was a quality player who was very valuable to the team. An ideal interchange player because of his versatility."

Drew Banfield

"Probably the most successful No.1 draft selection in history, certainly in terms of games played; no-one comes close. Won the 1996 club champion award and set a wonderful standard in terms of preparation."

Chris Judd

"I have only played a little more than two seasons with Chris, but that's as much as I played with some of our premiership stars. He is already a stand-out midfielder and has all the attributes to become a truly great player."

Phil Matera

"He has been the club's leading goal-kicker three times and, last year, averaged close to three goals a game, a great effort for a small forward. He also puts great defensive pressure on the opposition when they are trying to clear the zone."

Peter Wilson

"A hard-nosed ruck-rover who played in both of our premiership teams. Played well in the big games, particularly the 1992 grand final, and produced the highlight with that goal over his head in the last quarter. Very flamboyant."

Dwayne Lamb

"Was a player who set a wonderful level of professionalism in the early days. He wasn't overly tall, wasn't fast, was very left-sided, but still played 150 games; a great team man."

Ryan Turnbull

"Played as a ruckman in the 1994 premiership team and then held down centre half-back when I was recovering from knee surgery. Did a great job in both roles and was a little unlucky to miss a place in the 22."

The all-stars

GLEN JAKOVICH is an excitable bloke. You see it when he kicks a goal, when he plays in a premiership team, and when he plays for Australia. It was also evident as he looked over his selected team of all-stars that he has played with and against during his illustrious career.

"Have a look at that," he beamed. "Brownlow Medal, Brownlow Medal, Brownlow Medal, Brownlow Medal, Brownlow Medal, Brownlow Medal, Brownlow Medal, Brownlow Medal, Brownlow Medal (pointing to the names of Wanganeen, Crawford, Williams, Buckley, Hird, McLeod, Stynes, Harvey and Voss). Then you have the full-back of the century (Silvagni), two of the greatest goal-kickers in history (Lockett and Dunstall) and two blokes who have been hailed among the best of all time (Carey and Ablett).

"I played during a great era in the game and probably only appreciated how good it was after sitting down to select this team."

Jakovich's enthusiasm could not be contained as he gave a critique of each player selected in his team.

Gavin Wanganeen

"A wonderful player who has proven his durability over more than a decade with two clubs. Won the 1993 Brownlow Medal and has been a great servant of both Essendon and Port Adelaide. Reads the game brilliantly and has uncanny skills."

Stephen Silvagni

"Was selected as the AFL's full-back of the century in 1996. A close-checking defender who made it extremely difficult for his opponents to break free and kick goals. Was also capable of going forward and kicking a few goals himself."

Ashley McIntosh

"To my way of thinking, there was very little between McIntosh and Silvagni, with Ashley's reputation perhaps suffering a bit because he lives on the West coast and was only seen in Melbourne six or seven times a year. He had the same attributes as Silvagni."

John Worsfold

"An inspirational leader who was capable of playing on some of the biggest names in the game. Early in his career he was a hard working midfielder before sacrificing his game to play at half-back where the team needed him most."

Jakovich's AFL all-star team

Backs

Gavin Wanganeen   Stephen Silvagni   Ashley McIntosh

Half Backs

John Worsfold   Paul Roos   Glen Archer

Centres

Shane Crawford   Greg Williams   Peter Matera

Half Forwards

Nathan Buckley   Wayne Carey   James Hird

Forwards

Andrew McLeod   Tony Lockett   Gary Ablett

Ruck:	**Jim Stynes**	**Robert Harvey**	**Michael Voss**
Interchange:	**Garry Lyon**	**Jason Dunstall**	**Darren Jarman** **Paul Kelly**
Emergencies:	**Shaun Rehn**	**Garry Hocking**	**Guy McKenna** **Nicky Winmar**

Paul Roos

"When Fitzroy was struggling towards the end of its existence, Roos stood tall across half-back. Then he continued at Sydney and was a pivotal player in the Swans success in the mid to late '90s. Because he read the game so well, he was able to back his judgment and rarely made the wrong decision."

Glen Archer

"One of the toughest competitors you could ever play against. Imagine playing against this team as a half-forward and running into Worsfold or Archer! I reckon there would be a few blokes volunteering to play elsewhere on the ground."

Shane Crawford

"An inspirational leader for Hawthorn and a man with terrific skills on both sides of his body. So often, when the Hawks were in trouble, Crawford took it upon himself to dig them out of it."

Greg Williams

"I have never seen a player who operated better in the clinches. What he lacked in pace he more than made up for with his ability to read the play. His hands in close were as good as you will ever get. He had a bit of mongrel in him as well."

Peter Matera

"A wonderful player with explosive skill – it was a privilege to sit back across half-back and watch him unleash his own special brand of excitement on so many occasions. His performances in the big games set him apart from many others."

Nathan Buckley

"A polished performer who was finally recognised for his special abilities when he was a joint winner of the 2003 Brownlow Medal. Few players can boast the penetration and accuracy he displays with his foot skills."

Wayne Carey

"One of the great players of his time who probably deserved to have won at least one Brownlow. I obviously enjoyed some great clashes with 'The King' and saw first hand how good he could be, a fact measured by North's game plan revolving around his impact."

James Hird

"Another wonderful leader and a man who never seemed to be flustered. The best players always appear to have time when others would rush, and I never saw Hird make a hasty decision. Great poise, balance and presence."

Andrew McLeod

"In the mould of Peter Matera. He also has the attributes required to break open a game and uses them to devastating effect, evidenced by the fact he won two Norm Smith Medals. One of the most brilliant players I have ever seen."

Tony Lockett

"A brute of a man who was not afraid to use his bulk. Strong in body and a brilliant shot at goal, he gets the nod at full-forward just ahead of Jason Dunstall. He had two phases to his career, initially at St Kilda and then at Sydney, and the move north helped him become the highest goal-kicker in history."

Gary Ablett

"In a word, genius. He could do just about anything on the football ground – kick the mercurial goal, take the freak mark; he was a player who just had to be guarded for every second of a game."

Jim Stynes

"A remarkable and durable ruckman who successfully tackled our great game after converting from (Irish) Gaelic football. Holds the record for the most consecutive games and was the prototype of the new breed of athletic ruckmen."

Robert Harvey

"He was so strong through the hips that he was able to shake off would-be tacklers with ease. A great leader and dual Brownlow Medallist who would probably be even more highly regarded had he played in a premiership team."

Michael Voss

"Ranks as one of the most inspiring leaders of his era, captaining Brisbane in the club's hat-trick of premierships. A fearless competitor who leads by example and has done wonders for the promotion of our game in the Brisbane market."

Garry Lyon

"He could play with equal effect at either end of the ground and was a great leader at Melbourne. A gifted key position player, he had great hands and, like all the players in this team, he read the game brilliantly. I also had the pleasure of playing under him when he coached Australia."

Jason Dunstall

"A little unlucky that he played at the same time as the most successful goal-kicker in history (Lockett). But he was also a wonderful player, a deadly accurate kick and possibly a better team player than Lockett."

Darren Jarman

"Silky skills set him apart from most, playing in premiership teams with both Hawthorn and Adelaide. He was one of those gifted players who could really make a footy talk and had an uncanny knack of being in the right place at the right time."

Paul Kelly

"When you talk fearless, you think of Paul Kelly. A great captain at Sydney who led by his actions; he never left anything out on the park and drained every ounce of ability out of himself."

"Apologies to these players who narrowly missed selection: Shaun Rehn, Garry Hocking, Guy McKenna and Nicky Winmar. Rehn was a brilliant ruckman whose career was cut short by injury, while Hocking was as tough as they come. I had the privilege of playing alongside McKenna for much of my career, but couldn't squeeze him in, while Winmar, one of the most gifted players ever, was up against some all-time greats.

Epilogue

MY impending retirement at the end of the 2004 season will allow me to pursue opportunities in the business world, spend more time with my family, and indulge in my passion for fishing.

As I reflect on my career, I am truly amazed at how quickly it has passed. It only seems like yesterday that I was drafted by the West Coast Eagles. Yet, through the trials and tribulations of AFL football, the highs and lows of my career, I feel that I have given everything I could to the West Coast Eagles. I have extracted every ounce of blood, sweat and tears to make myself a better footballer, both for the team and individually and, in the process, became a better person.

I look back on my career and, apart from my late father Darko not seeing me play, I have no regrets. I hope that when he looks down on me from heaven he is proud that I upheld the family motto 'Sedulus et Audax'. That I have been zealous and bold for my team and my family on the battlefield that is AFL football.

Glen Jakovich